Find Lost Revenue

Uncover Hidden Causes To Common Sales and Marketing Problems

Patrick McClure
Mark L. Friedman
Judy Key Johnson
Philip A. Nasser
James W. Obermayer

Published by Solutions Press

Find Lost Revenue
Uncover Hidden Causes to Common Sales and Marketing Problems

Published by Solutions Press
4533 MacArthur Blvd., #200
Newport Beach, CA 92660

First edition printed February 2009

ISBN: 978-0-9752671-6-5

Printed in the United States of America

This is a work of non-fiction. The ideas presented are those of the authors alone. All references to possible income to be gained from the techniques discussed in this book relate to specific past examples and are not necessarily representative of any future results specific individuals may achieve.

Dedication

This work is dedicated to our spouses, Diane McClure, Flossie Friedman, Mark Johnson, Reed Nasser and Susan Obermayer, who heard the stories, were the echoes for solutions and lived with the results as surely as our clients.

The Authors

Additional Praise for *Find Lost Revenue*

"This is one book that every salesperson and business owner should have at their fingertips. It is packed with practical steps you can take to increase sales, today. These five seasoned professionals will show you where all the knobs and switches are to get your revenue machine running at full power. What an excellent resource!"
   Greg Bouwens, CEO, Knovolo Inc.

"*Find Lost Revenue* will give you 64 ways to improve your company's sales and marketing efforts, both immediately and in the long term. This is not just theory but practical information delivered by experts. It's a sales and marketing consulting project in a book."
   Roger Scherping, President, Fountain Industries Co.

"It has been proven that working harder alone does not produce sales results. So how does a sales person fulfill the dream of success? These five authors show how to find, and avoid hidden causes of common sales mistakes. This is a must-read for anyone who is in business."
   Missy Anderson, President/CEO, Connect The Dots

"Insights into sales and the selling process that are unparalled. This collaboration (of authors) represents an enormous amount of practical hands-on sales knowledge that yields tremendous insights. Highly recommended."
   Joe Chimera, President, The Shannell Group

"This book is unique in covering a wide range of sales and marketing topics with quick-read chapters, including examples and stories to reinforce the concepts, well vetted by the veteran writers who are experienced sales and marketing veterans themselves. I will make sure each member of my sales and marketing team uses this as one of their key resources for many pertinent issues that we face daily."
   Vane Clayton, CEO, KPA LLC

"If you are serious about deriving business from the internet, Search Engine Optimization (SEO) is not an option. It is a basic business essential. In our initial stages of redesigning our website, we met with two companies. One company said PPC was the way to go and the other recommended SEO. This book provided the basic data we needed to select the best option for us. We are enthusiastic that SEO will bring high quality leads, increasing our profits and providing greater web visibility for our existing and potential new customers."
   Rob Inman, President, Intelligent Power Solutions

Contents

Section One: Assessment & Analysis

Section Two: Strategic Sales Planning

Section Three: Sales Methodology

Section Four: Sales Management

Section Five: Training & Coaching

Section Six: Marketing

Section Seven: Internet Marketing

Section Eight: Business Development

Section Nine: Sales Lead Management/CRM

Section Ten:
Best Practices in Sales Lead Management

Preface

Consider the following recipe:
1. Take Four Men and one very Smart Woman
2. Over 150 years of Management and Leadership Wisdom
3. Fold in generous portions of time in the trenches
4. Add a touch of levity, a dash of sass, and a healthy dose of humility
5. Bake at wildly different temperatures in the School of Hard Knocks
6. Mellow with Judgment and Insight
7. Sprinkle with Random Flashes of Brilliance

You are now holding the finished product.

For the past year, these five management consultants, sponsored by Cerius Interim Executive Solutions, Inc., have presented a panel discussion, "50 Ideas in 50 Minutes," to numerous organizations and companies in southern California. These discussions, although focused on sales and marketing, frequently ranged into finance, operations, human resources, and information technology. In fact, there wasn't a single area of the organization they didn't touch.

These panel discussions were a hit. The five consultants taught each audience an incredible amount of information in less than an hour. They conducted spirited discussions with the audience and received feedback. This iterative process continued for over a year, during which the panelists frankly wondered whether they were teaching or learning from the audience. They concluded it was both. Collective wisdom has a way of rising to the top, just like cream above milk.

The process had one critical flaw, according to our audiences. Sometimes a great idea needs to be digested, considered, evaluated, criticized, and tested before it is accepted. We tossed out a lot of great ideas, one after the other, but the audience didn't have time to absorb the thoughts, much less mull them over. Members of the audience wanted to contribute their ideas as well. Again there simply wasn't enough time. Members of the audience wanted more content, more stories, more background, more facts...and there simply wasn't enough time. This frustrated the consultant panelists, who wanted to share the full richness of each great idea. They also wanted more time. What could we do to satisfy the needs of both audience and panelists?

We came up with a brilliant yet simple solution: Why not collaborate and write a book? Why not take the time to expand on our 50 ideas, put them down on paper, and publish it together? Why not give all of the existing and potential audiences what they have been demanding?

We decided to collaborate and publish the full story.

This time we'll take longer than 50 minutes. This time we're not limited to one minute per idea. This time we can fully explain what we REALLY mean and demonstrate why our ideas are critical to your success. This time, you, the reader, can take as long as you need to absorb these ideas and put them into practice.

We hope you enjoy our ideas. We forged them in the school of hard knocks and proved that they work time after time. You can read our biographies later in this volume, but suffice to say that none of us has made our career by sitting on the sidelines. None of us had time to specialize in theory, to spend time in the classroom. We worked in the trenches, dealing with customers, competition, partners, and processes.

By the way, don't expect us to always agree with each other. In fact, you might run into some conflicting ideas and downright disagreements! Remember, five strong minds are attacking common sales problems from different angles. Many times there are multiple solutions to a given problem. Sometimes the contrarian view is more correct. After all, when was the last time you experienced across-the-board agreement on ANYTHING in your company?

We dedicate this work to your success. If our ideas can help your company run better, if we can improve your bottom line results, if we can strengthen your competitive positioning, then our work is worthwhile.

Enjoy the book, and here's to your success!

Section One

Assessment and Analysis

Analyze what? Why?

Your sales team wants to sell, sell, sell! Great salespeople all have one trait in common: a bias for action! They hate meetings, they don't like to be confined to an office, and they abhor paperwork. If you want to drive them nuts, make them write reports all day or ask them for a strategic plan. They just want to get in front of customers and close deals!!

(By the way, if you DO have someone on your sales team that loves to write reports or do paperwork, transfer them FAST to HR or Operations. They'll never make it in sales.)

Sometimes things go wrong, terribly wrong. Sometimes the team doesn't get the job done. Sometimes management can't figure out what's happening and seems frozen in place. Sales is a complicated operation, with hundreds of moving parts. When it goes wrong the solution can be terribly difficult to figure out.

That's where Assessment and Analysis tools are worth their weight in gold! You can use them to uncover the hidden causes of lost productivity. They can help you assess what's working and what's not. Most important, they can lead you back to the holy grail of success.

Besides triage, management can also use these tools for advanced planning. After all, would you fight a battle without a plan?

In this section, we examine many causes of lost sales productivity. We also give you tools to get to the WHY of lost revenue. The faster you figure out what went wrong, the quicker you can implement a winning solution.

Stay out of the way of the thoroughbreds. You don't want to get trampled!

Chapter 1

How to Define SalesLeakage that Kills Sales Productivity!

By James W. Obermayer

"Me? My company? We're doing fine," the company president said. Then he looked up from his desk and asked, "Tell me again what you mean by SalesLeakage. We're making quota. Almost. I don't think we have any leakage."

"Maybe you don't," I said. "But most companies have it to some degree. SalesLeakage is like a dripping faucet. An occasional drip isn't too painful. However, a leaky faucet can waste thousands of gallons of water each year. Translate the leaky faucet to SalesLeakage from 25 or 30 points in your enterprise and you have enough accumulated leaks to prevent Sales from making quota."

"Give me some examples," the president said. "Just a few. Don't tell me that the salespeople need training. Everybody talks about training. I know we need more training. Tell me something I don't know."

That started the conversation, which led to the probability that there was enough leakage to cause a problem, just a few percent from many sources, a drip here and there on the wrong product or at the wrong time stolen from the bottom line. The lesson is that SalesLeakage drains sales and profits from even the healthiest organization.

A SalesLeakage search will find large and small issues that people know about but don't have the authority to fix.

SalesLeakage includes:

- **Sales competed for and lost.** Some companies track lost sales, some don't. Those that do something about the causes sell more than those that don't.
- **Incentive compensation failure.** If 70% or more of the sales force isn't making quota, your quotas may be set too high or the compensation program isn't providing an incentive. If the program has too many conditions, the incentive won't work with the compensation.

- **Time leakage for salespeople.** How salespeople use their time is stunningly simple to research and a bit more difficult to fix. OK, so it's very difficult to fix. Usually time issues with salespeople include their personal habits or problems with products among others. Chase it down and kill time wasting habits. The goal is always to increase the time spent in front of the customer selling.
- **Sales territory hemorrhaging.** Vacant sales territories cause more heartache than management wants to believe. For an in-depth discussion of this issue, see the chapter in Section Four titled: Why Vacant Territories Hemorrhage New Business.
- **Sales Inquiry Abyss.** See Section 9 for more on this issue.
- **Marketing failures to create demand based on quota requirements.** If marketing doesn't adequately understand its role, which is to create demand based on quota goals, salespeople will fail. I wrote a book on the subject called, *Managing Sales Leads: How to Turn Cold Prospects into Hot Leads.*

Some leakage is easily found; some takes time to search out with the help of sales and marketing personnel. The real issue for finding and fixing SalesLeakage is getting the commitment of the company president to get everyone working on the leakage problem.

Companies can do a leakage review on their own. If they know what to look for, they can find and address issues. When they do this, money drops more quickly to the bottom line and quotas can be met. Permanent fixes usually require the help of a consultant who knows what to look for so leaks can be stopped.

In a few weeks a professional leakage audit can search out and pinpoint the issues. The best way I have found to make permanent fixes is to build co-captained teams led by someone from a leakage expert and the marketing and sales management staff.

The teams work together to prioritize recommendations that bring the most immediate relief (60 -120 days). You can work out longer term leakage issues over time with teams of people most affected by the outcome. Follow-up quarterly meetings for a few quarters keep everyone on track and keeps SalesLeakage at bay.

As for the company president in our example, it took 90 days to find the leaks. No management changes were required but processes and procedures took some repair. It isn't difficult. Someone just has to make a decision that it's time to find the leaks and improve the sales volume along with the bottom line.

Chapter **2**

12 Reasons Sales Momentum is Lost: The Hidden Quota Killers

By James W. Obermayer

It starts with just a hint. One territory that you expect to make quota fails. You ask the usual question and get the usual rely, "I'll do better next month, some PO's are delayed, a run-in with a competitor, it's no problem."

But next month others come up with the same excuses and before you know the quarter is threatened and management is searching for answers. Pressure to produce moves into the field. Excuses abound. No reply makes sense. Just excuses. Something has stopped the forward momentum and no one can give you an answer that anyone can honestly believe.

Although the results are visible, momentum killers are difficult to identify. Ask the 2007 Mets what happened to their momentum. If you ask my sister Donna, the die-hard sports fan, the excuses are clear. A ballplayer here, a home office decision there, unseasonably warm weather, the rain, the presidential election, the economy, a player who lost his lucky charm or a pitcher that just couldn't do it. Take your pick, they lost the momentum.

Most often when there is a slowdown (euphemism for lost momentum), people blame an individual, competitor, or other nonsense. They seldom look inside to see what they may have done to kill the corporate sales momentum. While momentum killers can be internal or external, the self-inflicted wounds of an internal momentum killer can most often be avoided and fixed most easily when it happens.

Internal Momentum Killers include:
1. **Product failures:** If your product fails, you have high service costs. Salespeople try to fix something they didn't break and sales suffer. Jump on this one fast because it is possible to fix. I didn't say it isn't inexpensive to fix, but the lost sales momentum on a bad product and even other products in the line is too great to measure.
2. **Product Introductions:** (cause momentum on other products to fail). Related to item one above, product introductions (especially

7

premature intros) can cause huge disruptions in quota attainment. New products that eat up a lot of a salesperson's time can cause failures in other products that are supposed to be sold. If the new product is delivered late, the problem is compounded by drops in existing product sales, new product sales aren't delivered and counted and if the new product has problems it really gets ugly. I've been there and it was not pleasant.

3. **Management changes:** C Level, Sales Management and Marketing Management. Change coaches and watch what happens to the team. I am not a sports fan, but I remember when the LA Lakers had super stars wandering around bumping into each other until Phil Jackson showed up. When Phil Jackson left, they wandered, argued, gave excuses to the media, whined, and pointed fingers. It was embarrassing for grown men who played a game for millions a year to stand there without leadership and fail.

4. **Marketing budgets slashed:** Sales Lead Blackouts and Brownouts. This is a big silent momentum stopper, but few people blame cuts in marketing budgets for quota attainment failures. If you stop spending money on marketing and inquiries dry up, sales will slow down within a few months. Sales lead blackouts stop all media advertising and inquiries slow down and cease. Sales slow down three to four months later. This is a real momentum killer. Brownouts occur when marketing dollars aren't stopped entirely but are cut and fewer inquiries come in. Both ways sales slow and everyone blames everything else but the person who made the sales world stop by stopping advertising. Who was it that said that stopping advertising to save money is like stopping your watch to save time? It doesn't work.

5. **Sales Compensation changes or quota adjustments at mid-year:** If you want the salespeople wandering in circles for a month or two, change how they are paid or what the goals are for the year and momentum sputters until the salespeople get their bearings. If things aren't going well, don't significantly change the compensation program as a way out of the blind canyon. This is an amateur's mistake (usually suggested by the CFO or the president).

6. **Territory Realignments:** Change a sales territory for a salesperson and they will adjust over three to six months. Change many territories and watch while the organization slows to get familiar with the new responsibilities/territories/products. Don't do this at mid-year. If you have to do it, do it at the beginning of a year when these changes are expected.

External Momentum Killers include:

1. **Competitive Moves:** new products introduced that apply pressure to your own offering. Break-through products can cause sudden

increases in market share for the sponsor and sudden drops for you. This can include price drops by the competition. Can you fight it? Sure, with new products, lower prices, and an attitude that keeps you afloat until the competitor's product hiccups (20-30% chance).

2. **Sudden market shifts:** Gerald C. Meyers, author of *When It Hits the Fan, Managing the Nine Crises of Business,* nailed this one. Market shifts happen because of high gas prices or low gas prices or lack of supply or too much of something. Professionals generally see this coming if they know how to listen.

3. **Deregulation or Regulation:** Usually there are winners and losers when governments regulate or deregulate industries and products. Sometimes the benefits go to those regulated instead of the people or group that was supposed to benefit. Think of it as a game. If you are squeezed by legalities, remember that only time will tell if the intended consequences are to your benefit or not. Working with the new rules is easier than working against them. Find a way to adjust and move on.

4. **Public Perception:** Ask the Chinese how they fared when their products in 2007 were declared unsafe because of design. Whether they were at fault or the company that designed or specified the products screwed up, when public perception shifts against you, you need to move fast to correct it. This is one area of momentum loss that you can address if you move fast enough.

5. **Economic Shifts:** It hurts when money polices tighten, recessions take hold, the stock market drops, and purses tighten. This happens every five to seven years and most people weather it. You can use price and product features to get through these crises. Winston Churchill once said, "When you're going through hell, keep going." Get aggressive in tough economic times is sage advice. Advertise more. Create leads. It is more expensive, but aggressive people come out ahead in tough times.

6. **International Shifts in Markets (Marketplace or products):** Ask the Chinese (not them again?) how they liked it in 2007 when quality control issues surfaced. Regardless, the toy industry in China was hurt and American companies were scrambling for product. Was momentum interrupted? Ask Mattel.

I am sure if you give it some thought you will find other momentum stoppers you have experienced. Gerald Meyer's book, *When It Hits the Fan, the Nine Crises of Business,* is well worth reading and is the source of many of these momentum stoppers. If you see a momentum stopping event, work immediately to lessen the impact. Bring it up in meetings and ask, "Will this decision/event stop our sales momentum this year? What can we do about it?"

Chapter 3

GAP Analysis

By Patrick McClure

Consultants use many types of analysis, but a particularly useful one in understanding the sales organization is the GAP Analysis.

A Gap Analysis is performed to review and analyze current operational process and performance, determine the process and performance required to achieve a desired level, and develop and recommend alternative solutions to eliminate the gap between the current and desired position. A Gap Analysis examines three aspects of a business:

1. Current performance environment
2. Desired performance environment
3. Skills and processes required to implement the desired outcome

Let's use a typical example to illustrate the value of a Gap Analysis.

Situation: Client is complaining of a loss of sales productivity. Q3 was forecasted for $500K in revenue. The actual revenue was $300K. There was a $200K shortfall. Why did this occur?

Gap Analysis Methodology

First establish the baseline data to examine what actually did happen in Q3. During this phase, the consulting team works closely with management and key executives to develop an interview schedule and key questions for all stakeholders and key groups involved in the operation, internal and external.

During the data-gathering phase of a Gap Analysis, the consultants generally focus on the following areas:

Gap Analysis of Current & Desired Performance Environment

- Business environment and needs
- Product/service offerings
- Market position
- Core competencies/key values delivered
- Target markets

10

- Sales performance and analysis
- Distinctive capabilities
- Strategic business intent
- Desired level of performance and skills required

The original survey data is correlated and analyzed, comparison is made with industry benchmarks and competition, and the final report is prepared and delivered.

Let's suppose that the Baseline Data revealed the following results:
- The Product Line was changed at the end of Q2
- Key sales personnel were transferred to another project

Desired Performance Level

The next phase of the GAP is to determine desired performance levels. In this case, management had established a target of $500K in revenues for Q3 and an additional $800K in Q4, with annual revenues of $2.3 million for the unit.

Other parameters were established relative to product lines, sales organization, training programs, compensation, and bonuses.

Skills and Processes Needed to Implement the Desired Outcome

Once the existing and desired performance levels are subjected to detailed fact finding, it is possible to complete this phase of the GAP. A final report, prepared and delivered to the client, outlines the following:
- Develop and document the optimum selling process .
- Determine skills required for desired outcome.
- Determine the core competencies needed.
- Identify the organizational structure required.
- Recommend appropriate sales methodology.
- Recommend a program of training and coaching.

For instance, in the typical scenario we have been discussing, we might have made the following recommendations:
- Restore the product lines which had been eliminated.
- Adopt a firm policy to prevent mid-year product line changes.
- Transfer key personnel back into the unit and make them responsible for achieving the q4 number and the shortfall on q3.
- Establish incentives for these overachievers.

As you can see, the GAP analysis is a structured diagnostic tool. Its value is to systematically determine, from validated and audited data, the facts of the situation and to make solid recommendations to close the GAPS.

Chapter 4

Management Commitment to Planning and Process Improvement are Key to a Successful Sales Force Automation/CRM Implementation

By Mark L. Friedman

How many of you produce a product or service? How much time and effort did you put in to ensure that your manufacturing or service delivery process yielded the best quality product possible? You need to make the same commitment to spend a great deal of quality time to ensure your Sales Force Automation (SFA) or Customer Relationship Management (CRM) processes are best in class. Based on our experience and the survey work we have done we can confidently say the vast majority of companies have a "by the seat of their pants" approach to this critical business area. By spending the time to re-engineer your processes, you will provide a strategic differentiation for your company in the marketplace and increase the value of your company.

To maximize your enterprise's revenue growth and bottom-line by implementing a SFA/CRM solution, you've got to identify the business issues you want to address and begin to map out a plan to optimize them.

The best way to accomplish this is to conduct a comprehensive SFA/CRM-oriented assessment that will help you achieve greater clarity regarding what's important and where you should focus your SFA/CRM resources and investments. This approach will go a long way to assuring a successful outcome.

Such an assessment would measure gaps in performance and identify potential high priority SFA/CRM issues in the following 10 key areas:

1. Lead generation
2. Lead management
3. Opportunity management
4. Sales team efficiency

5. Sales team management and coaching
6. Marketplace intelligence
7. Order processing and fulfillment
8. Customer service
9. Customer service team efficiency
10. Customer service management and coaching

There are two ways to perform such an assessment. The first way is to interview selected members of the sales, marketing and customer service departments. Depending on the size of the company, you could interview everyone in these departments. As the company size increases, it is best to interview as many people as possible to ensure that all issues, off-line processes and requirements are successfully uncovered. This can take a lot of time and unless the interviewer is skilled and very structured, it might be difficult to objectively identify all areas of importance.

The second approach, especially valuable for larger organizations, is to conduct an on-line assessment that addresses each area above and request that all employees participate in their particular area of expertise. Larger companies typically specialize more than smaller companies. For instance, sales reps and marketing employees should answer questions about their area and customer service personnel should answer questions relating specifically to their area.

Using either approach results in a very important dividend: The participants will feel more committed to the end result program because their input was solicited.

Conducting the assessment will identify critical weaknesses and will help you to identify the process improvements that will be critical to your SFA/CRM success. It is important to note that some of the issues uncovered by such an assessment can be successfully addressed by improving process, some by customizing software and some by improving management and coaching techniques. All of these areas need to be evaluated and prioritized. A well-constructed assessment will give your team valuable guidance on what areas to address and their relative priority. Typical areas that are uncovered during this type of assessment are process deficiencies and productivity obstacles, incomplete, inaccurate, and inaccessible information as well as a lack of timely performance feedback.

Weaknesses in these areas can negatively affect your enterprise's ability to create demand for products and services, manage and qualify sales leads, close sales opportunities, process and fill sales orders, serve and support customers, and more.

Once management has agreed on the issues and priorities, it needs to assemble teams and assign them to come up with acceptable solutions. Be sure to include team members from each department that will give input to the process, actually perform the process, and receive the process' output.

When this is done, the chances of re-designing the process and identifying the complete information requirements are greatly enhanced.

Once the teams have completed their work and process improvement ideas have been identified and agreed upon, the company can then make sure these improvements are mapped onto their new software program.

Successfully assessing these important areas and improving existing processes and information flow will produce definite, dramatic improvements in sales and profits, and will go a long way towards increasing company value.

Section Two

Strategic
Sales
Planning

If you ever want to empty a room of sales managers, announce that you need them to work on their strategic plan. WHAM, there they go out the door, along with most everyone else in your company.

Why this aversion to planning?

Most likely your sales team has had very bad experiences with the planning process, such as irrational targets, unrealistic expectations, ridiculous assumptions, unworkable plans, and idiotic strategies.

Let's face it. Most often a "strategic plan" is cooked up in the dead of night by the executive team and gets handed down to sales management with the instruction to "get this done or else." Any input submitted by sales management to the strategic plan somehow gets deleted or changed. Any disagreements or requested changes are similarly ignored. Top down management rules!

It doesn't have to be that way! Strategic planning, done correctly, can energize your organization and motivate your sales team to consistently overachieve. When the planning process follows simple logical rules, it can be vastly successful. A good plan will also keep you on track to meet your goals and help you to avoid all the potholes, bumps, and hitchhikers along the way.

We all know you can't achieve your objectives without a plan. You can't keep firing at targets that are unknown or poorly defined, especially when you don't even know what gun (or bullets) to use. You won't be able to attract the kind of talent you need to staff your organization if you don't have a clear idea of where you're headed. You certainly can't assemble the troops and lead the charge if you don't have any defined goals and objectives.

This section gives you some great tips on putting together sales plans that work!

21st Century Sales Platform

Chapter **5**

Do You Have a Sales Plan?

By Philip A. Nasser

Your sales team has just completed a fiscal year with good performance. Your boss is happy...therefore, you are happy. You learned some things, did some things well, made some mistakes, grew the business and, overall, feel good about what you accomplished. The new fiscal year is here and you may be asking yourself, "What am I going to do to move closer to our objective of excellence? How do we get better?" Do you have a plan to answer these questions?

Many managers start over. By that we mean they assign new quotas, make territorial adjustments as needed and make a few deployment adjustments with available manpower (key accounts, alliances, customer base salespeople, outbound telemarketing) and move onto the next twelve months. This approach has worked in the past, why should it be changed?

"If you don't know where you're going, any road will get you there."
Alice in Wonderland by Lewis Carroll

Sales plans are like business plans in one important respect: you must have one! We can almost guarantee your performance will be better with a sales plan. You will also create focus and efficiency. A good sales plan will:

- Provide specific actions to help you achieve your objectives
- Keep your sales team in alignment with key company/team goals. Having all team members pulling in the same direction is a requisite for success in business
- Keep you and your sales team focused on the correct targets, i.e., prevent the waste of precious resources on actions and programs that do not support next year's goals
- Identify key success factors (ksf's)
- Provide a rationale for assigning key tasks to team members
- Provide you (and anyone else who may be interested) with a detailed roadmap of what is to be done and by whom

18

- Leverage your company and team strengths
- Help beat competition

Through the course of our work with clients we have developed a sales plan template that has proven effective. We recommend key members of the management team participate in the development of the sales plan. While you may want to include additional items or delete some items, following are the main components of a sales plan for almost any sales team.

Executive Summary

This section includes an agenda and a summary of the main points of the sales plan. It should be a high-level summary and be no more than one or two pages long so that a senior executive can read it quickly and understand what you are trying to accomplish.

Business Objectives

This section contains the sales mission (high-level statement of the purpose of the sales force and the basis of its competitive advantage), key objectives and goals for the coming year (revenue targets, strategic and tactical goals, and any planned key changes).

Current Sales Situation

This section is broken into three parts and provides the basis, justification and rationale for the strategic positioning in the next section.

The first part is a review of the highlights of the previous year with particular attention paid to strategic achievements. Included here would be key achievements and a brief explanation of why they occurred. Examples are number of new accounts, new business vs. sales to existing customers, improvements in recurring revenue, changes in client size, wins vs. competition, market share, and close ratios.

The next part reviews the lowlights of the previous year. Included here are the key shortcomings and a brief explanation of why they occurred. While this section can be painful to review, it has the benefit of helping focus on areas offering potential for improvement and frequently points to areas that, once improved, offer significant payback.

The third and final part of this section is an opportunity statement. It includes strengths, weaknesses, risk assessment (threats), and opportunities for coming year. Given the highlights and lowlights, where is the best opportunity for the sales team and company in the coming year?

Strategic Positioning

Considering the findings in the sales situation section above, the strategic positioning section deals with identifying where the best market opportunity resides (which of the market segments offer the most potential given your differentiators), which channels of distribution to use and how competition can be eclipsed, neutralized or controlled. This section will also highlight your company's value proposition and competitive advantage and how they will be used to achieve company and team goals.

The market opportunity portion simply states where the best growth opportunities exist. This section will include such items as an assessment of macro environmental factors (political, industry merger and acquisition activity, social/cultural), economic factors (capital markets, scale of operations, inflation, recession, exchange rates for global operations), industry trends, effects of new technology, trends in key accounts, new markets, new products, competitive changes, sources of leads, and new business for coming year and strategic alliances.

The channel of distribution portion focuses on the desired mix of revenue between direct, OEM, and indirect channels. This topic is included in the strategic positioning section because the mix of revenue is so tightly tied to profit margins and any imbalance can cause a shortfall. For instance, it is possible to exceed revenue goals and miss gross margin targets because of an improper revenue mix.

The last portion of the strategic positioning section deals with competition in the industry segment being served. Positioning differs if you are one of the key players in the market or if you are a new entrant. What action has the competition taken that requires attention and action? This section asks you to define your competitive advantage and how it will be used to eclipse, neutralize or control competition. It is common to list key competitors and describe how you plan to prevail over each of them.

Sales Objectives/Forecast

This section lists the key targets (e.g., new accounts, market segments, gross margins, penetration percentages, alliances, etc.) to which the sales unit is committed. It is advisable to include a time-phased forecast of revenue that includes the channels of distribution along with an explanation of how the forecast will be achieved. Detailed breakouts by customer, product, market segments, and alliances within each channel of distribution are very desirable to ensure everyone has full visibility to the revenue source.

Key customer revenue and plans are included in this section as well. It is common for a few customers to represent a sizeable portion of a company's revenue. Therefore, it is very desirable to provide visibility to the total revenue from each key account, define who is responsible for achieving it, and list any special resources being deployed.

Sales Model

In growing or changing companies or where new products are being brought on-line, it is advisable to use the sales model section to demonstrate how, for instance, the effective execution of a newly deployed sales methodology will support the achievement of sales objectives. Which control and measurement metrics will be used? Who is responsible for summarizing and reporting? If appropriate, what is the contingency plan?

Timeline

This section is most useful when new revenue streams (acquisitions, new products) are planned and where there is some uncertainty as to when the revenue flow will begin. Contingency plans to accommodate a short-fall in revenue are included in this section.

Key Success Factor (KSF)

This is the most important section of the sales plan for the manager and executive because it lists the top three KSFs that, if achieved, will guarantee achievement of the plan. One of my managers used to refer to these as the "critical few," which emphasizes their absolute importance.

The KSFs are developed after considering all the foregoing sections of the sales plan. Based on an analysis of the preceding sections, what must the unit absolutely do to ensure success? While the KSFs can exist in many areas of a manager's operation, this section highlights them, puts them at the top of everyone's priority list and ensures that the necessary resources are applied to their achievement.

Chapter **6**

How to Predict the Number of Inquiries Required to Make Quota

By James W. Obermayer

Whether you are a sales manager who needs to predict how many inquiries you need from marketing to make quota or a marketing manager required to take a sales goal and turn it into the number of inquiries you have to generate, the formula is the same.

Quota $/ASP/45%/Market Share % = Inquiries.

For instance:

Let's say you have a $10 million dollar quota, an average sales price of $15,000, and a market share of 25%. If you have 100% follow-up of the inquiries, this is the number of inquiries you will need to make quota.

$10,000,000/$15,000/45%/25% = 5,926 inquiries.

This formula can be used for any product that has a sales forecasted dollar number. If you follow-up on only 50% of the inquiries, expect to need double the inquiries to make the quota number.

A savvy marketing manager will look at each product that has a quota and then use the formula to calculate the gross number required. From this point forward the confident marketing manager breaks down the big number into smaller chunks based on the lead generating tactics they have available. Let's assume that the marketing manager has to create 5,926 inquiries for a single product.

Lead Source	Number of Inquiries Required
Trade shows Three shows, 500 inquiries each	1500
PR Six press releases, 100 inquiries each	600

Direct Mail	
Four campaigns, 20,000 mailed, 2% Response	1600
Web Pay per Click	1200
Directories (four)	600
Web "Contact Us" Page, 100 a month	1200
Total	6700

This is more than the sales manager needs to make quota, but then everyone needs a hedge number. Producing nearly 800 more than required is just good business sense.

The marketing manager's next goal is to create a consistent, month to month inquiry flow (avoiding blackouts and brownouts). Blackouts happen when inquiry flow totally ceases for a few weeks or even several months. Brownouts occur when there are dips in sales inquiries of 25%-30% below the 12 month average. Ideally the marketing manager will produce 558 inquiries a month. A nice even flow, right? Well, it's a start.

To do it right the marketing manager has to ask the sales manager what type of a sales ramp he is expecting in the coming year. If the sales ramp is flat the sales manager has to bring in $833,000 a month and the marketing manager 558 inquiries. But most sales managers will tell you that sales will grow as the year progresses. The marketing manager should be able to take this into account when they create the inquiry flow. Most will ramp up inquiries as sales ramps up.

This timing can be worked out with sales management. Some of the timing issues have to do with the sales team's ability to consume inquiries and not waste them. Marketing management may have to deal with seasonal shifts in buying patterns (selling to school districts for instance), when trade shows occur. This is a nice problem to have. To start with, just get marketing to agree to create a specific minimum number of inquiries to help the sales department make quota. The rest will come naturally.

Chapter 7

The Rule of 45:
Predicting Sales Results From Inquiries

By James W. Obermayer

The Rule of 45 is the basic measurement premise from which you can measure the effectiveness of virtually all lead generation programs. It is a steady, reliable rule which simply says that 45% of all inquiries (not just qualified sales leads), will buy from someone. The time frame for this purchase is usually, but not always, within 12 months. Your own market share is projected as a percent of the buyers. I have been involved in over 100 Did You Buy Studies on a variety of products and the Rule of 45 is consistent.

If you follow-up on 100% of the inquiries, the biggest variable in this formula is the time needed to reach the 45% threshold. Every product has a typical average time frame for the majority of the interested parties to make a decision. For consumer products this could be a few months, for B2B products the Rule of 45 is completed within 12 months.

On average the following rules apply:

- Within three months 10%-15% of the business to business prospects will buy someone's product.
- Within six months 26% will buy someone's product.
- Within one year 45% will buy someone's product.

While time is a pacing item, the most influential issue for a company to attain its fullest share of the marketplace is salesperson follow-up. Follow up only 25% (a consistent number I hear from many companies) and you'll only compete in 25% of the available deals.

How important is this variable? The following example shows what happens when sales follow-up dips to 25%. First, let's look at the potential in a group of 1000 inquiries if follow-up is 100%.

1000 Inquiries X 45% = 450 potential buyers

Times follow-up of 100% and you still have 450 buyers

Times 25% market share = 112 buyers

Times ASP (average sales price) of $10,000 = $1,120,000 in sales

Reduce the follow-up to 25% and this is the result:

1000 inquiries, x 45% x 25% follow-up x 25% x $10,000 = $280,000

Pretty brutal, isn't it? You spend 2%-20% of yearly revenue on marketing. Because of poor follow-up your sales will be 25% of what they could have been. This calls for a mandate from sales management: 100% sales inquiry follow-up is part of every salesperson's job description. It can be a condition of employment.

Chapter **8**

Why Marketing Blackouts and Brownouts Kill Sales Growth!

By James W. Obermayer

We walked down the long hallway to the sales manager's office when he stopped and pointed to a chart on the wall. "That," he said, "is the problem. Sales in Q1 were fine, right on track, but in Q2 we started to weaken and Q3 we hit new lows. We're dying and I have run out of reasons." With that we continued walking to his office.

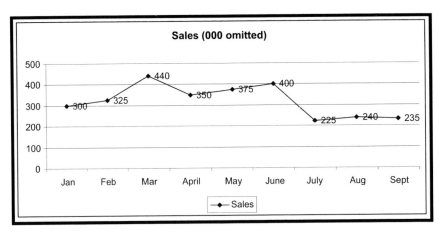

The first quarter grew, the second quarter tried and faltered and Q3 dropped further and was flat.

As we passed a doorway he motioned, "That's the director of marketing's office." And just outside the door, on the wall was another chart.

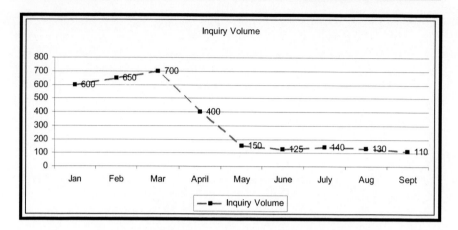

Sales inquiries started their precipitous decline at the end of Q1.

I stopped in front of the chart and looked while the VP of Sales continued, then stopped and came back to me. "Oh yeah," he said, "And on top of it all, the lead volume is down." "Just a moment," I said. I went back down the hall, took the sales chart from the wall and brought it up to overlay on the sales inquiry chart. "That's the issue," I said. "Yeah, I know the leads are down," he grunted.

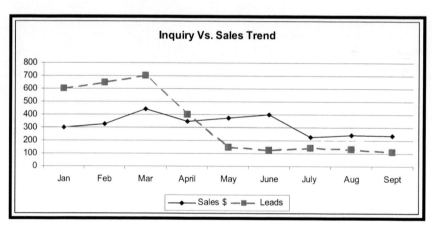

This is what the two charts, sales and inquiry volume looked like when overlaid on each other.

"What you are missing," I said, trying to lessen the blow of the obvious, "is that three months before your drop in sales the inquiry volume dropped. He had a sales inquiry blackout. While he was aware that the inquiry count was down, he was only vaguely conscious that the two were intimately connected to each other. A blackout, I explained, was a sudden drop in sales inquiry volume. A brownout is simply a lesser but still noticeable reduction in inquiries sent to salespeople.

I have found that the first place to look for the reason behind a dip in sales is the sales inquiry volume in the months running up to the sales failure. If there is a dip in sales inquiries, it is usually because someone has asked marketing to reduce spending. When the marketing budget is cut, for the first two or three months sales continue to grow because salespeople drain their immediate pipeline. But when the pipe has been used up and is no longer growing, sales begin to drop. Within the next three months sales volume is in a tail spin until it levels out to reflect the new realities of fewer sales inquiries and salespeople who are now almost going it alone. Demand creation drops and sales drop.

For this company, when we built the inquiry volume back up to historic levels to support sales growth, sales climbed and the company emerged from the blackout. Unfortunately, the cost in lost sales, plus a few sales territories that lost salespeople because they couldn't make a living and quit, was expensive. It took three months to rebuild the inquiry volume and sales started to rebuild three months afterward as the pipeline got fatter. Altogether it took nearly a year to get back to where they were in sales growth. In the meantime they lost salespeople and gave several million dollars to their competitors.

The lessons are:
1. Inquiries build and sustain a pipeline.
2. By substantially reducing sales inquiry volume, a Blackout or a Brownout can lead to sales reductions within three months.
3. It takes six months or more to rebuild a pipeline once it has been depleted.
4. A three month drop in inquiry volume will lead to a year's losses in sales growth.

What so few managers suspect but fail to heed is that sales and marketing are in an elegant dance together. The lead in the dance is marketing, which creates demand. Sales only take the lead when it must, when marketing fails to build demand. Do not let inquiry volume drop.

Chapter 9

Get Rid of Your Excel Spreadsheets... and Start Tracking Marketing ROI

By Mark L. Friedman

Many sales forces we work with have streamlined the administrative and reporting requirements for their sales reps. While there may be other reports to fill out, most require an expense report and a forecast report. It was interesting to note, in our recent survey of small to medium sized companies, 43.8% of respondents indicate they create their sales forecast reporting in Excel.

Don't get me wrong. Excel is a fine product and keeps track of this information easily. This approach, however, has several fatal flaws:

1. It makes the sales organization less productive.
2. It creates additional work for either the administrative staff or the sales management.
3. The information is not readily available to the rest of the organization on a real time basis.
4. It separates the sales lead record from status reporting and makes ROI reporting practically impossible.

Let's discuss these flaws in more depth and see how a well executed Sales Force automation (SFA)/Customer Relationship Management (CRM) approach successfully transforms this broken process.

1. What typically happens in Excel-driven forecast reporting environments is that sales inquiries and leads are sent to the sales organization in several ways, typically email, voice mail, and fax. The sales rep receives the lead and contacts the account. The reps work the lead and keep notes in their individual systems (manual, Outlook, personal contact manager, etc.) about the contact, action items, and when to call back.

Once a week or once a month, the sales reps have to stop selling, review their notes or recall from memory the status of the account. They then create or update their individual forecasts in Excel and send them to either the sales manager or an administrative person. To accomplish this, the sales reps stop their most productive activity: calling on and selling to qualified accounts. The more time it takes to fill out the spreadsheet, the less productive the sales organization will be. In addition, reps are working with three separate systems: email, the reps' contact management system, and the Excel system. There's a lot of room for error.

2. The sales manager or the administrative person then copies and pastes the information from each sales rep into a single spreadsheet and reconciles any column inconsistencies. This time-consuming, ultimately VERY unproductive process is a big waste of time, especially if the sales manager is doing this work. It also takes time away from potentially valuable coaching, managing, and selling. The administrative people could use this time more effectively for other company projects as well.

3. These finished forecast spreadsheets are sent to each person or department that needs the information. They end up at each individual's desktop. If one person makes a change on the final spreadsheet, the process has to start all over again.

4. By requiring the use of Excel to create a forecast report, the company creates a new, off-line process that continues the strategic disconnection between the actual lead, which was probably received as a text-based email, and the reporting of the status of that lead. Without a significant investment in human (read: sneaker net) and financial resources, it is virtually impossible to track the original source of the lead.

By properly planning and then implementing an SFA/CRM solution, each of these problems goes away. Two main areas must be addressed to fix these fatal flaws.

1. Deliver all leads to sales within the SFA/CRM software

One of the big mistakes companies make in setting up their sales lead management systems is to create a qualified sales lead and either fax or email it to the ultimate lead owner, the person actually tasked with making contact with the account. Once a company embarks on this path, it quickly loses control over the process. Pieces of paper get lost and if the lead information is re-entered into the SFA/CRM software, much of the original information captured in marketing will typically not be re-entered. Only the basic information a sales rep needs to contact the account will make it back into the software.

Best practice calls for the company to enter all inquiry and qualification information, including lead source information, into the SFA/CRM software. Once it is determined that a lead should be sent to sales, the software should be set up to accomplish a few fundamental steps:

1. Assign a lead to a specific sales rep.
2. Distribute the lead to the assigned sales rep.
3. Notify the sales rep that they have been assigned a new lead.

Most SFA/CRM software can handle these steps easily, including creating a new task or email within the application. If yours doesn't, then request assistance from your reseller to incorporate this functionality into the software. You can always send a fax or email that a new lead has been assigned to the sales rep, but it is critical that the sales rep retrieve the information within the SFA/CRM software.

If this is not done, it creates a strategic disconnect between where an inquiry/lead came from and which accounts from these lead sources actually resulted in revenue and profits. Once lost, it is practically impossible for a company to recover this information. This disconnect will deny the company critical information needed to manage sales.

2. Create all forecast reporting in the SFA/CRM software

In order to recreate forecast reporting in the software, Sales needs to document and agree upon the sales stages they use to close business. These stages must be clearly defined so everyone in the sales organization knows what they represent. This will result in more uniform and consistent forecast information. Once this is done, the SFA/CRM software can be modified to collect this information and create on-line, real-time forecasts. With proper training and management oversight, sales reps should update the status of accounts as they call on them.

Finally, tell Sales that sales forecast reports will only be accepted from the SFA/CRM software. NO EXCEPTIONS!

When the system is set up correctly, sales reps will spend less time updating the software than they spent creating or updating the Excel forecast. This can result in significant productivity gains. In addition, having this information available on-line and in real-time will greatly reduce the number of phone calls to sales reps requesting current lead status. This will result in higher productivity and fewer interruptions for both the sales rep and the sales manager.

By implementing the SFA/CRM software as described, a company can track Marketing ROI more effectively. By allowing marketing access to the lead status reporting, they can create sophisticated ROI reporting based on the lead source and the sales forecast information. Marketing can determine which programs are working and which are not. They are in a better position to justify spending money on proven successful programs that generate more and better leads. This typically results in marketing being able to allocate their budgets more effectively and even justifies spending additional money to execute productive marketing programs. This has a positive impact on the ability of sales to hit their assigned quotas.

Section Three

Sales Methodology

It may sound strange, but there is a method to our madness.

Trying to get a group of salespeople and managers to work together can sometimes become downright impossible! We are dealing with a multitude of "D's", including:

- different ages
- different sexes
- different ethnic backgrounds
- different languages
- different skill levels
- different training levels
- different motivations

Further, salespeople as a general breed are thoroughbreds. They like to overachieve and become the star of the show. They like to do things their way. They are independent, egotistical, pushy, and sometimes arrogant. Your company absolutely DEPENDS on them, doesn't it?

How do we get them all working together toward a common goal? How can we induce them to work together as a team?

The answer is sales methodology. If you can get your sales teams to understand and agree upon a methodology, your success is assured. If not, you'll soon start to feel like you're herding cats. Or being herded by cats!

This section will explain the critical role of sales methodology in creating your success.

Chapter 10

All Sales Methodologies Work

By Philip A. Nasser

Webster defines methodology as "the science of method, a system of methods." Certainly a sales methodology includes a science and a system. But what exactly is a sales methodology? When we use the term we are referring to:

- A method of approaching, engaging, and qualifying prospects with the goal of reaching mutually-beneficial business outcomes
- A process that encompasses everything that occurs from the time a prospect is identified until there is a happy, referenceable, repeat customer.
- A process that builds a value chain for all activities the sales force engages in during a prospect's buy cycle
- A best-practice that teaches the core competencies required in all sales value-chain activities

You may ask, "What sales methodology should we use?" Or possibly, "What sales methodology is the best?" Most professional sales consultants recommend that you employ a sales methodology. Clearly, it is better to have a methodology than not to have one. However, how do you tell the difference between them and decide which is best for you?

In this chapter we suggest that those are the wrong questions. They're wrong because the popular sales methodologies (Strategic Selling, Collaborative Selling, Profit-Improving Selling, Target Account Selling, Solution Selling, Value-Based Selling, and many more) work. While they all work, they might not be appropriate for every company. Since they all work, it doesn't matter (almost) which one you choose. The systems are not difficult to understand. They all have value and utility.

A better question is this: How do we implement and manage the system we choose? This is the area most companies have problems with.

Companies squander valuable assets (time and money) on sales methodologies. After the fact, management asks, "What happened? How did we spend all this money and get so little in return?"

Each methodology includes a high-level template and rationale for its selling process. There are differences between the products, of course. For instance, Target Account Selling has a good political module, Solution Selling's discovery model is easy to understand and use and Power Based Selling introduces us to the Fox. Each of these systems is unique, but they all work.

In another chapter we explain why you should customize sales training to your company's particular needs. Sales methodology should be customized as well. A company should take advantage of the best practice methodology and customize it to their unique needs. Don't confuse customizing your sales methodology (which is recommended) with the unique challenge of implementing the methodology successfully (which is extremely difficult). The first attempts to get the highest value for your company via a customized methodology. The latter recognizes that, no matter which methodology you choose, the critical path to success is implementation and management.

Unfortunately, as good as these systems and technologies are, companies have difficulty implementing them successfully. While there are several reasons for this, the most important is the difficulty associated with making the necessary sales and management behavioral changes.

Here is what you need to do to ensure the successful implementation of your chosen sales methodology:

- **Executive Management Commitment**: As with almost all strategic initiatives, if the highest-level operating executive does not squarely and publicly support the new system, disappointment with the results is likely. The greatest likelihood of success occurs when the CEO or the highest level executive will:
  - o Commit to the success of the project and explain why it is strategically important to the company
  - o Prioritize the necessary resources and ensure they are available for the project
  - o Give as much visibility to this commitment as possible. The more, the better. Company meetings, newsletters, and other informal company gatherings are good platforms to deliver the message
  - o Provide the necessary "change management" resource to the implementation team
  - o Check on the status of the project on a frequent basis, asking for updates and inquiring as to what resources are necessary to make the project a success
- **Operating Management Responsible for the Implementation**: Once the "corner office" is behind the project, the management

team responsible for the implementation must get "on sides." This group will:

- o Understand the methodology and participate in its customization. This work, which should be done very early in the project, will ensure the methodology accommodates the unique characteristics and quirks of your company's channels and sales process.
- o Be the first group trained on the new system
- o Be ultimately responsible for the rollout and installation of the new process with all users
- o Understand how and why the new system will improve the results and increase the productivity of the sales team
- o Know how the new system will be deployed in the various channels of distribution
- o Understand clearly their role in the implementation and be prepared for some reticence from the salespeople
- o Need measurement and monitoring tools that tell them where they are in the implementation process. These will include activity management tools, key-account reporting, and win/loss reporting.
- o Understand they are the first line of offense/defense and be ready to support the effort on all fronts
- o To the extent customers and prospects will be affected, take responsibility for explaining the benefits to them
- o Take responsibility for leading regular, periodic progress reports for the various teams/groups involved in the implementation
- o Be responsible for developing and managing action items to correct any misdirection in the project

We believe that if you are able to accomplish these items, your sales methodology implementation will be very successful indeed.

Chapter **11**

Different Prospects Buy
Different Kinds of Value

By Philip A. Nasser

"The advice of their elders to young men is very apt to be as unreal as a list of the hundred best books."   *--Oliver Wendell Holmes*

My first sales manager was Tom Jensen. He was a tall, tanned, good-looking, charming, tough Korean War Army veteran. I learned a lot from him. I remember Tom once telling me that we needed a slightly different approach to the sales call depending on who we were calling on. I listened but did not understand. Certainly, prospects were different, but weren't we selling them the same products? Wouldn't they all be interested in the same features and benefits of our products and services? Maybe, I thought, Tom meant we had to be sensitive to the different backgrounds and experience of each prospect, such as where they went to school, and what they liked to do in their leisure time. Rather than ask for clarification (and, in the process, show my ignorance), I just nodded. Note to self: try to figure out what he's talking about.

After all, we had completed over a year of company training that focused primarily on our great products, how they worked, why they were the best, and how customers benefited by using them. Wouldn't the value be the same regardless of who the prospect was? Seemed logical to me. It was tough enough getting out into the territory and making the required number of calls, presentations, and demonstrations. I truthfully didn't want to take time to delve into the subtleties Tom was trying to teach me.

It wasn't until several years later, after many successes and disappointments, that I began to understand what Tom was talking about. It wasn't until still later, when I had been promoted into a sales management position, that I began to appreciate the brilliance of understanding exactly to whom you were selling. It took some stern lessons before I got it.

38

"Perception is reality" started the breakthrough in my sales thinking. How does this relate to sales, you may wonder. Let me pose this question: when you are calling on a prospect, who are you actually speaking to? A CEO, CFO, CIO, CMO, a VP of Manufacturing? No. You are speaking to all the other party's life experiences. In a fundamental way, we consist of all we have seen, read, and experienced. The same is true with prospects. We all form decisions based on our experiences and perceptions.

Early in my sales career, I remember frequently commenting under my breath (especially about prospects who were well qualified but seemed to be stuck in indecision) "How come they can't see our solution is superior? I can see clearly how they would benefit. Why can't they see it? Why are they not fighting to change their current system and make a decision in favor of us?"

The reason? The prospect's perception was different than mine. They did not see the "clear values" I saw. They had a different perception of the situation, were coming at it from a different starting point, and did not see the value I saw. Perception drives value. I still had work to do with these prospects because they did not understand how they could improve their operations (improve profit) by using my products and solutions. They were not fully qualified.

Yes, they had a need and I knew our solution could solve their need. However, they did not perceive it the way I did. I needed to get "into their moccasins" to understand where they were coming from and supply additional information (facts, references, proof, etc.) to help them change their perception. Until I learned to get our collective perceptions in line, my forecast was full of prospects who were qualified from my standpoint (had a need we could provide a solution for) but seemed to be stuck in a mode of indecision or no decision. They were just not motivated to move.

How do you get your and your prospect's perception in line with one another?

1. Learn the general orientation and interests of the various functional positions in the companies to whom you are selling. This is a matter of perspective.
2. Perform discovery (from the prospect's perspective) to define the key drivers of profit in each functional area of your prospect's business. This is most often a matter of understanding what each functional area does to increase the organization's profit.
3. Verify the prospect's perception. In other words, ask if they would share their perception with you. This is so obvious it is often overlooked. Just ask.

For CEOs, CFOs, CIOs, CMOs, and VPs of Manufacturing, let's take a look at methods of keeping perceptions in alignment. What are the likely general orientations and interests of each of these positions? What are the values that drive their decisions in their roles in the corporation? What processes can you improve for each functional area? How do you verify that perceptions are in line?

Chief Executive Officer

CEOs are interested in these topics:

- Revenue growth
- Return on investment
- Sustainable competitive advantage
- Distinct competencies
- Success for the company and themselves
- Staying ahead of competition
- Measurable, tangible results (bottom line)
- Company image

Before you talk to a CEO, learn how your product or service will help in one or more of the areas above. If you have a meeting scheduled with the CEO but do not know what areas you are going to explore, postpone the meeting until you do.

For instance, if your prospect is known for excellent customer service and your product/service can help them build on that competency, you have a subject area in which to ask a few questions in an attempt to establish value (and get common perceptions in line).

Chief Financial Officer

Areas of common interest and orientation for CFOs are:

- Cost reduction
- Margin improvement
- Efficiency improvement
- Expense control
- Improvements in monthly roll-ups, reporting and closings
- Analytics

While one might expect that everyone in a company is interested in revenue growth, this is not the top area of responsibility or primary interest for a CFO. They are, however, very interested in squeezing cost out of the operation, improving margins, and efficiency. They are interested in any tools that will help them better analyze their operations (financial and otherwise).

In what ways do the products and services of your company improve the operations and processes of the CFO? How do they provide the CFO with better information to make better decisions? While most firms' financial processes are the same, exceptions exist. Learn how each prospect handles things before you advocate a solution. It is difficult to recover after making a recommendation that is inappropriate for a prospect. It is much better to have done a thorough analysis in advance of offering solutions to issues.

Chief Information Officer

Areas of interest and orientation for CIOs are:

- Security. With systems, servers, databases, and data centers spread literally all over the world, security is at the top of the list of importance and interest. The internet, electronic commerce, nomadic salespeople, and telecommuters have all increased a company's security risks.
- Fail-safe-solutions
- Redundancy
- Technological developments in any of the above areas
- Cost reductions

At one time all data and equipment resided in the data center at the company headquarters, where it was secured and bunkered. That is no longer the case. Now data and information assets are spread all over the world. Security is the top CIO priority. While the VP of Sales might be interested in sharing information with alliance partners or opening up offices on two or three new continents, the CIO will not be as excited about these projects unless there are assurances security will not be compromised.

In what ways do the products and services of your company improve the operations and processes of the CIO? How do they provide the CIO with improved or solid security or with better information to make better decisions or provide them with additional cost savings? How do the processes of this particular department differ from others with which you have worked? How do those differences affect the recommendation you make to improve operations?

Chief Marketing Officer

The top marketing executive is interested in:

- Demand creation
- Branding
- The most efficient way to go to market
- Channels of distribution
- Company image
- The weaknesses and actions of competition
- The latest trends in industry marketing

Marketing executives almost always feel they need higher budgets to meet their objectives. They ask for more funds to support advertising, direct marketing, collateral, trade shows, product marketing efforts, and competitive intelligence. Therefore they will be interested in anything they can do to stretch the effectiveness of any of their programs.

In what ways do the products and services of your company improve the operations and processes of the CMO? How do they provide better information to make better decisions? Or provide them with cost savings? Or, for instance, give them improved return on investment on marketing campaigns? How do the processes of this particular department differ from others with which you have worked? How do those differences affect the recommendation you make for improvement?

VP of Manufacturing

The person responsible for manufacturing operations will be interested in and oriented toward:

- Efficiency
- Just-in-time inventory management
- Total quality management
- Six Sigma
- Process improvements

If a key initiative of the company is quality, the VP of Manufacturing will be much less interested in cost control than methods to improve quality, much less interested in internet security than just-in-time inventory management, and much less interested in revenue growth than improvements in process efficiency.

In what ways do the products and services of your company improve the manufacturing operations of the prospect? How do they provide the VP of Manufacturing and his staff with better information to make better decisions or provide them with cost savings? How do the manufacturing processes of this particular prospect differ from others with which you have worked? How do those differences affect the recommendation you make to improve operations, increase supply chain efficiency, lower costs, quicken time to market, improve service or increase efficiency in other areas?

When you recognize that different prospects buy different kinds of value and focus on perspective, process, and verification, you will remove uncertainty, lower anxiety, and improve both relationships and results.

Chapter 12

Profits are the Only Advantage

By Philip A. Nasser

"If you want to make small improvements, work on behavior and attitudes; if you want to make major improvements, shift your paradigm (how you see the situation and your role in it)."   *--Stephen Covey*

Mack Hanan was one of the first business authors to develop a solution selling methodology in his book *Systems Selling Strategies*, published in 1978. The book centered on the idea that a winning sales strategy needed to wrap your product or service in other products or services that you, the systems seller, would deliver or ensure were delivered. These other products or services focused on the prospect's processes, suppliers, and customers, anything to help the prospect run his business better. Taken together, this total solution provided an improved Return on Investment (ROI) for the prospect.

According to Hanan's formula, we must, first and foremost, become experts in our prospect's business. This strategy was particularly helpful if you had a commodity product because you could "expand" the product to include other products or services.

If we attained this expert status, we could help our prospects improve their business processes. Before we could do that, however, we had to know how our product or service helped the prospect improve their product or service and in the process improve their profit. This was, for many of us, a breakthrough in sales thinking.

After all, up to that time, our companies had spent considerable time and valuable resources teaching us about our products--their features and benefits--so that we could demonstrate these capabilities to prospects. Before we were allowed to go into the field, many of us were required to attend product training school. Everyone at the training got immersed in the product(s) and what it (they) could do. The thinking was we only had to be experts in our product, which was viewed as the most important factor in making us successful. Yes, we had to learn some qualifying and closing skills, but they, too, were focused on our product or services. Along the way we were also taught competitor's weaknesses so we could "knock-off" the competitor if necessary. Essentially, however, our training was inwardly focused on our product and its capabilities.

It was as if customers bought our products based on the product capabilities alone. It was because we had faith that "if you build it, they will come." So you can see that Hanan was opening new, career-changing, doors for us as he asked us to shift our focus to the prospect's business. We had to re-work our thinking about how we approached prospects. In fact, we had to re-work our positioning with the prospect. We could no longer think of ourselves as peddlers of product, we had to position ourselves as profit-improvers. In truth, the ideal positioning for any salesperson of any product or service is that of "profit-improver."

Hanan's idea of becoming an expert in a prospect's business contained a valuable gem which was hidden deep in the system. It was initially overshadowed by the immense, seemingly insurmountable, difficulty involved in actually becoming an expert in our prospect's businesses. For sales forces that were vocationalized (calling on a particular vertical market, for example), the task was somewhat easier since they called on prospects that were typically in one industry. For those salespeople who called on many industries, the task was a lot more forbidding.

It actually took a year or so for those of us who were trying to implement the system to understand the little secret. Before I reveal that little gem, let me ask you a question: Why do companies purchase capital assets? Or, purchase anything for that matter? Why do companies purchase your products or services?

After all, if companies didn't spend their funds on your product or service, if they were able to keep their funds for themselves, they would be able to increase the retained earnings capital account and improve their balance sheet. There would be more funds available for dividends to stockholders and owners. Wouldn't that make the investors and owners happy? Not necessarily. Investors and owners would not be happy if the company did not continue to grow the business's revenue and profits.

As we have learned through the years, a company cannot stand still. It is either growing or shrinking. There is no middle ground. All companies have to grow to survive. If a company is not growing, its income statement, cash flow and balance sheet come under pressure. There are few long-term strategies (actually, none I know of) for success for a company whose revenues are shrinking. Yes, there are cash-cow strategies, but the end game usually finds the company out of business or absorbed by a competitor. In sum, companies have to spend to grow.

"Why do companies purchase anything?" Here are a few of the many reasons:

- Help fund growth and additional volume
- Develop new products

- Gain a new group of customers
- Provide a new capability-inventory control, better supply chain, better reporting, customer relationship management, etc.
- Improve efficiency and accuracy
- Eliminate errors
- Save labor
- Have better information to make better decisions
- Gain a competitive advantage

All the foregoing is true but doesn't tell the whole story. Here is the real reason companies spend their money: ***in all cases, in all events, without fail, companies purchase/invest (in anything) to improve profit! And there are only two ways to improve profit: increase revenue or lower costs!***

Let that sink in for a minute. Do you mean that trucks, machinery, software, supplies, buildings, and inventories are all purchased to improve profits? Yes! Does that include the product or service you sell as well? Of course! At bottom, companies invest money to make money. Everything they purchase is intended to help them improve profits. Otherwise, they wouldn't invest it. There are plenty of alternative places for prospects to invest their funds. And you can be sure that, if there is a competing investment that provides the same outcome with a better return on the investment, it will receive funding before a lower-returning project will. For any company, profits are the only advantage. Technology, for instance, is not an advantage...it is a cost.

Therefore everything we can do to help our prospect improve their operation/processes endears us to the prospect and, importantly, separates us from our competitors who are simply trying to "sell product." Profit-improvers are clearly differentiated from their competitors. Understanding this enabled us to change our positioning with prospects. It enabled us to get "in the prospect's moccasins" and to "get alongside" the prospect to jointly solve a problem. We all agree that if a prospect views us as trying to help improve their profits...rather than simply trying to sell product...we become allies, not adversaries. The "win-win" concept gained new meaning once we understood that we had to become profit-improvers.

In summary, if prospects purchase your product to improve their profit, you had better know how your product will be used to improve your prospect's profits. In other words, it isn't enough to know how your product works; you need to know how it works in the larger context of a prospect's operation to improve profit. That is why we say for all companies and salespeople "profits are the only advantage."

Chapter 13

Why Prospects Stop Talking to You

By Philip A. Nasser

"The greatest revolution of our generation is the discovery that human beings, by changing the inner attitudes of their minds, can change the outer aspects of their lives."   *--William James*

The deal was proceeding well. We had just presented a large draft proposal and the prospect seemed to like it. The proposal listed the various components of our offer in an "a la carte" format so the prospect could pick and choose the items he liked. He commented that was just the way he liked it. We had hoped to get a commitment to start the project immediately at the end of the meeting, but the prospect said he wanted to review the proposal over the weekend. When we asked if there were any questions we could answer while we were together, the prospect said, "No, I just want to review the proposal and talk to my team."

While the outcome of the call was not perfect, it was clearly heading in the right direction. We shook hands as we left and said we would call the following week. In the prospect's parking lot we felt pretty good but were careful not to congratulate ourselves because, after all, we did not have a signed agreement and deposit check. Nevertheless we thought the deal was good enough to forecast a close the following week.

Guess what? The prospect did not return our call the following week or the week after that. How could that be? After all, we presented what the prospect wanted, in the desired format, the prospect had given us buying signals throughout the proposal presentation and there were no objections.

Sound familiar? This happens more often than we want to admit. Does the prospect tell you why? Probably not. And for good reason. If we have done a good job in the pre-sale environment, prospects end up liking us and don't want to hurt us. They particularly don't like to deliver bad news to us. If they are not ready to make a decision or are favoring a competitor, they can go into a non-communication mode.

We will explore the causes for this in a minute, but first, think about your forecast. How much of your pipeline is in a delayed mode? If you are like most, it is easily between 30% and 50%. Wouldn't it be great if you could reduce the percentage of deals in this condition? To do this, we must understand the cause.

Here are the five most common reasons a prospect stops talking to us:

1. **Lack of connection to a critical business issue.** If we haven't determined how our solution will help them improve profit, reduce costs (or provide improved customer service), we can expect a delay. Unless our discovery process identifies, and we have the prospect agree upon, major inefficiencies in their operations that our solution will remove, expect a delay. Senior executives only spend/invest in areas that have the potential to positively impact their business. By asking appropriate questions, we can learn why the prospect has gone mute. Why can't you solve this issue with resources inside your company? What is the real value of this solution? Why are those problems important to you? Who else is affected by these issues? Why would that matter to you or any other executive?

2. **Lack of perceived value.** While closely related to the first reason, value is different enough to stand alone. Once we have found the critical business issue, we have to establish the value of improving it in the prospect's mind. Most people can only juggle five or six critical issues at a time. We all live with problems that we don't need to solve today. It is no different in a business. Resources are only applied to the issues offering the greatest payback. Can our prospect articulate the value or impact of addressing the business issue? If our solution, from their perspective, doesn't have enough value to get in their top five or six, we can get put on the back burner. Perception is reality. If our prospect doesn't perceive the value of our solution, we are probably in a delay and have more work to do. If we don't know, ask the prospect to quantify the impact of resolving the business issue. Better yet, ask how the solution will impact them personally.

3. **Out of sync with the prospect's buy cycle.** This may be the most common reason prospects stop talking to us. Here is how it happens. We have a monthly, quarterly, and annual quota. It is a bad strategy to try to close all your business in the last month of your fiscal year. We need to close business every month. The "quota clock" ticks incessantly and can captivate our consciousness. It can be all-consuming...especially when we are behind quota on a year-to-date basis and our boss wants to know when we're going to get on plan. Therefore, we want and need to close business all the time.

Our prospects, on the other hand, are driven by a completely different clock. Every department and project in their company competes for limited resources. Typically they check internal resources to see if they are able to meet their need internally. If not, they make a decision to go outside their company for help.

Prospects will typically review and evaluate several options. Depending on the size of the deal and how mission-critical it is, they may even ask a consultant to help in the evaluation and selection process. If our prospect has a bad quarter, all capital expenditures could be frozen. Other activities (merger, acquisition, diversification, executive turnover, divestiture, etc.) have the ability to halt or eliminate our deal. We are unable to control any of these issues. All we can do is make sure our sales efforts are in sync with the prospect's buy cycle and make sure we allow them to complete the steps in their purchase process. Closing too early can create problems that are difficult to overcome.

4. **Decision authority.** It is important to determine whether the person we're in contact with has made this type of decision before. When and how? Triangulate this information by asking these same questions to multiple people in the organization in order to find out who really has the decision making power in the organization and how purchases of this nature are made.

5. **Risk.** Over the course of a sell cycle, risk moves up in importance in every prospect's mind. Selecting a new vendor or a new solution involves risk. The prospect's perception of risk can span issues like lost time or money, or personal ramifications such as career or reputation. As a prospect gets closer to making a decision, the risk becomes greater in their minds. Common tools for alleviating risk include happy references, trial programs, demonstrating credibility with ironclad implementation plans, guarantees, and backing from executives in our firm.

Chapter 14

Why You Should Sell High, Deep, and Broad

By Philip A. Nasser

"The important thing is to not stop questioning. Curiosity has its own reason for existing."   *--Albert Einstein, 1879 – 1955*

Early in my sales management career, we were working on the largest deal in the company's history; one that would help the company finish the fiscal year in a strong fashion, make the 100% Club for the salesperson on the account and help my branch office reach its objectives. The prospect was the largest service organization in our city with over 200 service technicians in the field every day. They were wholly owned by a large electronics firm in the same city but at a separate location.

Our key contacts in the prospect's operation had been the General Manager and his staff, whose offices were on the north side of town. They assured us that getting our agreements signed would be a formality after they had reached an agreement with us. While they didn't have signing authority, they had approval authority. The GM and his staff said they were keeping their "bosses at headquarters up to date on the project each step of the way." "Will we need to meet the headquarters people?" we asked. We were told that would not be necessary.

After all, the headquarters CFO, VP of Manufacturing, and IT staff were working on a major upgrade to their computer systems and were deep into that project, which had issues of its own. When we persisted and asked to meet the CEO, they told us there was no chance we would ever meet with him and that the CFO of the parent company would approve the deal. All we had to do to win the contract was convince these divisional people that we could do the job. We were suspicious but decided to take the chance and concentrate on helping the division solve their problems.

The prospect's main concerns were with their service operations. Their business was growing at 20% per year and they were just adding people to an already inefficient system, making it even more inefficient. They knew their work flow was very inefficient and that installing a well-designed automated system would increase efficiency and customer service at the same time. A two for one. It was obvious to them that they would be able to squeeze much inefficiency out of their operation and that would cost-justify any system that would help them do it.

The key decision-making criteria, which the prospect had openly shared with us, were to be able to schedule service calls efficiently so the technicians would spend as little time as possible on the road between calls, bill and collect for the service call, keep track of truck inventory, and incorporate an incentive system into the service call scheduling system. We were replacing a manual scheduling system and the accounting that had been processed on an old bookkeeping machine. While we would install an accounting system to handle purchasing, payables, receivables, and general ledger, we were told there was no need to interface with the accounting systems at the headquarters operation.

After reviewing their current operations and processes, we confirmed there was considerable value for the client if they were able to meet the stated objectives. The benefits of automating the scheduling system were enormous since it was estimated each technician would be able to make at least one more call per day, possibly two. The only variable costs associated with the additional calls were gasoline, wear and tear on the vehicles, and replacement part costs. The rest of the additional revenue would flow directly to the bottom line. The prospect could make up to 400 additional service calls per day with a small increase in marginal costs. Additionally, it was estimated that the number of service calls handled by the in-bound telephone operators could be increased by 20-40%, giving our prospect the option of reducing staff or growing the business without adding additional staff. Lastly, they were experiencing unexplained inventory shrinkage. It was thought the technicians were helping themselves to whatever they wanted on the truck or in the company stores, but, since the tracking system was faulty, there was no way to prove it. Savings in inventory alone would amount to over a hundred thousand dollars per year. The General Manager, who was paid on the net profit of his division, was excited about the potential.

We worked for several months on the deal. This required multiple calls and demonstrations with multiple prospect and company people defining the scope of the operations and the cost of the software modifications necessary to meet their needs. The prospect told us early on that competition had been eliminated from the deal. Our optimism increased the longer we worked on the deal. As the end of our fiscal year approached, we kept asking the prospect if we would get the deal done in time to get the agreements signed. We were given assurances that we would.

During the last month of our fiscal year, after modifying, reworking, and discounting our proposal several times, we presented our agreements, which had been modified, reworked, and discounted several times, to the General Manager. At that time he gave us a piece of bad news. He told us that, without his knowledge, the scope of the computer systems upgrade at headquarters had increased and might now be expanded to include all of our prospect's service operations and accounting. At a minimum, it would handle purchasing since both companies bought from the same suppliers and there were quantity discounts available if the purchases of the two entities were combined.

We were crushed. In any event, we could not get our agreements signed until the feasibility study at headquarters, which was being conducted by IBM, had been completed. IBM also would be supplying the hardware and software for the upgrade. The headquarters CFO had convinced the board of directors that his upgrade project was more important than ours and, while he thought the work our company had done was beneficial, he saw greater value integrating the systems of the division into headquarters. (Read that: he was better able to cost-justify the project to the board if it encompassed the operations of both entities. The funds earmarked for our proposal would be totally or partially saved and included in his upgrade project).

The CFO was assuming (erroneously, as it turned out) that the systems at headquarters would be able to perform the operations we had proposed for the service division. It was eighteen months before we got any business from the prospect and it was a much smaller piece of business than originally proposed. Why did it take so long? Because IBM kept adding fear, uncertainty, and doubt to the prospect's mind by intimating they would be able to meet the needs of the service division. IBM had access to the ultimate decision-maker, the Controller. We did not.

Key Take-Away

What is the key lesson from our experience? What actions might we have taken to secure a better outcome? First let's answer the question "What is the major issue with this prospect?"

As it turns out, the division we were working with was unable to influence the behaviors of their headquarters personnel. They wanted our solution but were unable to convince headquarters personnel to accept our proposal. At the same time we were working with divisional personnel, the folks at headquarters were working on initiatives that were basically opposed to what we were trying to accomplish. What started out as a simple upgrade proposition at headquarters turned into a much larger integration project involving processes at the service division that was our prospect. While we were working with division personnel to meet their needs, the upgrade project at headquarters was growing in size and scope. So, what might we have done differently?

Confirmation (get it in writing). Anyone who has spent time and energy trying to manage the behavior of prospect personnel knows how frustrating that activity can be. As much as salespeople try to convince themselves to the contrary, prospects are going to do what they believe is in their best interests. They will not do solely what is in the salesperson's best interest.

Prospects only look to outside solutions after they have exhausted their investigation of internal resources that could be used to solve the problem. Even if a prospect decides to look outside of their organization for a solution and later finds out there are internal resources that can be used to solve the problem, they will almost always exercise the option to use internal resources. As Sharon Drew Morgan argues in *Selling with Integrity*, salespeople build their credibility by actively encouraging their prospects to look inside their organizations for a solution before investigating outside alternatives.

In actuality, the only things that can be managed and controlled by salespeople in the presale environment are their actions. That doesn't mean there aren't tactics that will improve knowledge and information. It just acknowledges the fact that controlling prospect behavior is not reasonable or even possible.

To deal with this reality in larger sales, we encourage our clients to have their prospects sign a "Project Evaluation Process" document, or something similar. This tool enumerates the dates and times of the typical steps leading up to a decision and confirms the prospect's participation in the steps. Included are items such as discovery meetings with key prospect personnel, proof of concept, demonstrations, existing customer visits, a review of legal agreements, and, finally, execution of the agreements by the prospect. It is important to allow go/no go decisions at several points in the timeline.

Please note: this document must be signed by the signing authority (the person who will sign the agreements, the person with ultimate decision-making authority). In the case of our prospect above, the document would have been signed by the corporate Controller.

The benefits of using a tool such as the Project Evaluation Process are:

1. The steps in the client's analysis and buying process that lead up to a decision are confirmed.
2. All parties agree on their individual responsibilities during the process. This is very reasonable. After all, this is a business arrangement and most prospects understand and respect a salesperson's need to confirm the actions and expense incurred by each party in the process. Prospects have told us they wish their salespeople used a qualification tool like this one.
3. Access is gained to the ultimate decision maker. Without using a tool like this access is frequently denied.
4. With access to the decision maker, other needs and requirements can be uncovered and relationships can be built.

5. Objections are uncovered and can be dealt with up front. What is better than learning about a prospect's objections at the start of a sales process? Would anyone rather wait until the end of a sales process to learn of important objections?
6. The deals in the pipeline will be better qualified! We have not had a client or salesperson who was not interested in improving the quality of their pipeline.

What if the prospect will not grant access to the ultimate decision maker? This is a critical question because the answer is, if a salesperson is not able to gain agreement on the work that will be done by both parties leading up to a decision, they are best advised to leave the prospect and move on to a better one. Leaving a prospect is an unnatural act for a salesperson, but our experience shows that when salespeople start saying no, their sales increase. It is counterintuitive, but it works. In the case of our prospect above, the time and resources spent on the deal would have been much better spent on another prospect.

We believe the biggest mistake made by salespeople in larger sales is not being able to walk away from a deal early if they are unable to meet with corporate approvers. Why don't salespeople ask the tough questions of prospects? Because they don't want to hear the answer! They don't want to endure the possible rejection. They believe that given sufficient time, with good attitude and effort, they will win the prospect over to their side. They believe this because they:

- Have confidence in their abilities
- Believe they will win the deal (actually, the best salespeople believe they will win all deals)
- Can see how they will be able to solve the prospect's problems
- Believe they can change prospect's thinking
- Have large egos
- Don't have other prospects to work on
- Have to meet a quota
- Can't afford to pass up any prospect who might buy
- Want to have something to include on their forecast to management.

While one or more of these may sound reasonable, not one of them justifies spending valuable time and resources on prospects that are not properly qualified.

Chapter **15**

Six Tips to Make Quota the First Month of the Year: Or Chase the Numbers All Year Long

By James W. Obermayer

Maybe it was while I was on the strategic planning staff of a Fortune 500 Company that I noticed that across the five sales forces, if the salesperson/region made their quota for the first month of the year, then making the quarter was almost assured.

If the salespeople make the first quarter, making the first half became much easier. Yep, you guessed it, if you make the half, making Q3 is almost assured. Once Q3 is made, the year isn't far off. In fact, as a sales manager you can take a vacation, come in late, and leave early during the last quarter because the momentum build up will take you through to a great finish.

Of course, I have seen and experienced exceptions (see the chapter on the 12 reasons Sales Momentum is Lost). Life and the marketplace can get in your way, but for the most part, once momentum has its way, the year will be made.

Ok, you say, so how do I make this happen? At the end of every year we have drained the swamp and there is nothing left for Q1. We have SPIFed our way to success[1] and January often appears to be a dry month.

There is something you can do as a sales manager to keep up the momentum so that January isn't as dry as Death Valley in June.

Keeping the Momentum for a Great First Month - Actions You Can Take

1. Promotional activities that generate demand in Q3 and Q4 must never slow down. Because inquiries and sales leads have a life of twelve

---

[1] SPIF is defined as Sales Performance Incentive Fund

months, as long as you keep promotional activities at a peak in the last two quarters of the year your pipeline will not be drained.

Much depends on the length of your sales cycle, but with cycles between three and nine months, by creating a strong backlog of demand, your pipeline will not be drained and you have enough to work with.

You will have to train marketing and marketing communications to keep up demand and not allow budgets to be raided.

2. Think of having a special quota attainment bonus for the first month of the year. Create excitement in your team and competition between the salespeople to start off fast. Too often everyone is so weary after the finish of the year just past that they start with a slow pace in the first two weeks after a year end. Some take vacations; others stare at the phone as if they never want to pick it up again. "No one wants to hear from me for a few weeks," they'll say as they get caught up on paperwork. Nonsense. Shake them up with a fast start. Remind them that the time to pounce is when the competitors are asleep. Teach them that competitors will often get a slow start to the year because they are infected with the SS Virus (Slow Start Virus) that you had last year. Schedule a sales rally-kick-off meeting or conference call at 8 AM on the first morning of the first day of the new year.

3. Promotional activities in the first month must be aggressive and outrageous. Marketing must be on-board to buy into your momentum building right at the beginning of the first month. Give them new leads and new reasons to talk to prospects. Nothing excites a sales force than to have the phones ring. Challenge marketing to make it happen.

4. No vacation time in the first month of the new year for anyone in the sales department. They will complain but love you for it later. You need everyone jumping on the month. You don't want 20% of the available sales power absent while you are trying to make the month (which makes the first quarter).

5. Make sure there are no vacant sales territories at the beginning of the year. I know, easier said than done. Maybe you want to weed the garden a bit after the year finishes. I hate to tell you, but you should have done that earlier. Minimize open and uncovered territories as much as possible. Hire and train in the last quarter of the year and get those new people into the field.

6. Don't have the traditional sales meeting in the first month of Q1. Avoid taking everyone out of the field for what will amount to at least a week (yep 25% of the sales time in a month), when you are trying to build extraordinary momentum. Have the sales meeting later when momentum has been achieved.

I am sure, if you think about it, that you'll find other momentum building ways to have a good first month of the year. Just think how sweet it will be when you pull it off and going into the second month you are ahead of quota. How sweet it will be!

Chapter 16

If I Could Show You a Way

By Judy Key Johnson

Back in the good old days, when employees joined major corporations assuming lifetime employment, those companies reciprocated by investing heavily in employee training.

For eager young college grads and MBAs selected for the IBM training program for the high-end products, the Data Processing Division, sales training meant two years of classroom work in the IBM education centers in Endicott, New York, Chicago, and Dallas, coupled with an internship program.

Ask any IBM sales alumnus, such as me, what the toughest part of the program was and the answer is likely to be the same – the practice sales call. We dreaded making those pretend calls on our instructors, sometimes in front of the class. There was an IBM way, and we had to use it.

The most sacrosanct part of the structured sales call was THE QUESTION. If you didn't use THE QUESTION in your practice call you would flunk. Even as we learned more and more over the two years of training, we always had to invoke THE QUESTION in our call.

THE QUESTION we had to ask our hypothetical buyer was, "If I could show you a way (to do something) then would you (take a committing action)?"

At that time, having never sold anything in my life, I had no idea that what they were teaching, or rather forcing, us to do was to:

1. Qualify the customer
2. Advance the sales process

The Qualifying Question

Most salespeople share common personality traits – outgoing, socially skilled, and highly verbal. They can talk and listen as well, for a long time about most topics – sports, restaurants, and, yes, about their products and why they are superior to the competition. They can even talk about return-on-investment and the reasons for buying now.

However, many salespeople, especially those who are inexperienced or who have never been properly trained, avoid the less comfortable part of their job, which is asking tough questions one-on-one about whether the prospect is actually willing and able to buy.

To avoid wasting your time as a salesperson, you need to qualify the customer and the sooner the better:

- Is their role in the company such that they are in a position to advance the sales of your product, if not as the buyer, then as the influencer or coach?
- Is the organization itself in a position to buy within your time frame?
- What are the conditions such that, if you the salesperson meet those conditions, that prospect will take action such that the sales process will be advanced?

What can the prospect do for you?

There are two parts to THE QUESTION and each part requires knowledge of the customer.

1. **"If I could show you a way...?"** In order to ask this question, the salesperson needs an understanding of what the prospect values. Is the prospect looking for a technology solution to a problem, "If I could show you a way to transmit large streams of digital data to your subsidiary in Singapore without needing to install a receiver in each remote location...?" or an economic solution, "If I could show you a way to finance your new equipment without drawing down your line of capital...?" You need to know what is important to that prospect professionally and undoubtedly personally as well. There is generally a political and or personal component to any sale, looking good to the boss or solving a problem that someone else was unsuccessful in resolving.

    It's so much more difficult to know what the prospect wants, really wants, than just to ramble on about your product and the latest sports results. In using the first part of this question, the salesperson is required to listen, and think, about the customer environment and the prospect as an individual.

2. **"...then would you (take this action)?"** Everyone you are talking to should be able to help you advance the sales process in some way. They may be a source of information, a coach, an approver, or the buyer. This second half of the qualifying question forces the salesperson to understand how that person can help you ultimately get the sales. When you make what you are asking for clear, it is much more likely to happen. You are making a deal with them – IF I do this then you do that. If they agree, then once you hold up your part of the deal "If I could show you a way..." then it's their turn to hold up their end of the deal. Because you have previously asked

the qualifying question, they have already agreed that they will take that action and they know exactly what that action is.

The action may be something as simple as setting up a meeting with their boss, "If I put together a custom demo using the data you have provided, will you get your boss to attend?" Or it may be with the approver, "If the return on investment, using your numbers, is less than nine months then will you recommend this software in the next budget cycle?"

Training Tool

Most sales planning sessions do an excellent job of categorizing different individuals in a target company by their roles, using the jargon of the preferred sales methodology (Spin Selling, Solution Selling, Miller-Heiman).

There is often a concerted effort to identify the value proposition by role – the CFO is interested in financial value, the operating chief in productivity, and the section chief in meeting budget.

Use of the qualifying question takes these two pieces of analysis – role + value – and focuses on the result that should advance the sales process. "If I (the sales rep) could show you (*role*) a way to achieve (*value*) then would you do (*action*)?

role + value = advancing the sales process

It's a great achievement for one not-so-simple question.

Section Four

Sales Management

Recipe for disaster: Promote your finest salesperson to the role of VP of Sales. Don't replace him with another accomplished salesperson. Find out after six months, when the entire organization has disintegrated, that your newly-promoted VP of Sales has no idea how to manage other people. He has no aptitude for it and never had any management training.

Does this sound familiar?

We see this sad scenario repeated over and over across corporate America. It happens so often that we have to wonder what some people are motivated by. Do they intentionally set out to destroy their entire revenue stream, or is it just accidental?

Here's Rule #1 about sales management. Sales ability has absolutely nothing, repeat nothing, to do with management skill. In fact, it's quite rare that a sales superstar will make a good sales manager. Think about it. Your great salespeople are closers! They hate being cooped up in an office, they hate working with spreadsheets, and they detest meetings. Why would you want to promote them to manager and force them to do everything they hate?

Fortunately, there are dozens of excellent people who can be trained to become good sales managers. There are tools available to manage the sales pipeline, systems available to provide structure, and processes in place to integrate all aspects of your customer relationships. If you're lucky, there may even be some management training thrown in for good measure.

Effective sales management, as this section will explain, can be studied and understood. The fundamentals and best practices can be grasped and implemented with great success.

Have courage! There are answers to the many problems of sales management!

Chapter 17

Fundamentals of Sales Management (For Entrepreneurs)

Or
"What I always wanted to know about sales management but was too busy to ask."
The Role of a Sales Manager

By Philip A. Nasser

"The waste of life occasioned by trying to do too many things at once is appalling."   *--Orison S. Marden*

If you have been a sales manager responsible for the sales performance of others, you can appreciate the intensity and pressure that goes with the position.

Here are a few examples that will give those who have not been sales managers a feel for what we're talking about:

> Your days are full of activity (i.e., no time for planning during business hours); meetings are lined up back to back; customers call demanding (and deserving) help with an issue; salespeople call from prospect or customer offices with issues and questions; (you make a note to spend some skill-building time in the field with the rep that just called); your boss calls looking for help with (pick one) budgets, an unhappy customer, forecasts, accounts receivable, getting product shipped; other employees come to you with personal issues that require attention; suppliers call asking to schedule some of your time; prospective employees need to be interviewed; Human Resources calls with concerns about your favorite candidate to fill the open position; marketing calls wanting to know what happened to all the leads they sent you last quarter; product marketing calls to review the launch plan for the new products scheduled for release next quarter; your lead salesperson tells you he is being courted by your top competitor and that they

are offering a big salary increase and an equity opportunity; your presence is required to help close a big deal; your lawyers call and tell you there is a problem with the big contract you turned in last week; the Controller calls asking for your quarterly budget update---and this is just the first day of the week!

While no two days are alike for any sales manager (truly a blessing), they all resemble the day above in speed and intensity. At the end of the day when you ask yourself what you accomplished, the answer is often not very complimentary. Most of us know we need to work "on the business" not "in the business" but struggle to find time to do so. Such is the plight of sales managers, especially those in growing companies with growing sales forces.

Here is the truth: in the midst of all this flurry you need to manage and plan. You may have read an article or book on management effectiveness that said, "Managers with clean desks were more effective than those with cluttered offices." As you recall this, you self-consciously put a pile or two of papers in a file cabinet drawer and ask yourself, "Where do I get the time to do what I know I ought to be doing?"

Now the big question: What is a world-class sales manager supposed to be doing? We have found the work can be broken into four categories: recruit and retain, teach, coach, and motivate. Let's take a look at each one individually.

1. **Recruit:** Before you can assemble a good team, you need good players. Since recruiting is such an expensive exercise (locating candidates, screening candidates, deciding on the best candidates, checking references, and putting together compelling offers of employment), you would expect companies to have well-defined systems to support this important task. They don't. Best practice in this area includes seven items:
   a. Define the ideal candidate
   b. Develop a position description
   c. Identify likely sources of candidates
   d. Build a sales candidate model
   e. Develop interview focus areas
   f. Develop interview questions
   g. Check references

   For a detailed discussion of each of these items, see the chapter titled *Seven Steps to Recruiting the Best Salespeople.*
2. **Teach:** If the early period of training for an employee is not conducted properly, outcomes will suffer. It is impossible to overemphasize this point for, if employees are not properly prepared for success, the company, the customer and the employee are underserved. For new employees, training in the sales process, industry, product, and competition will occur shortly after hire. It is

at this time that knowledge and understanding grow, expectations are set, and the ground for success is laid.

Before good coaches put their teams on the field, they review with the players and other coaches the overall objectives for the team. This may include the rationale for offensive and defensive schemes and an explanation of why this will allow the team to win. Play books are handed out. Plays are diagrammed. Roles are explained. Individual expectations are made clear. Homework is assigned. The importance of physical conditioning is stressed. Competitive weaknesses are reviewed.

Notice the heavy emphasis on teaching, both physical and psychological, before the team actually gets on the playing field. This metaphor applies almost perfectly to a sales manager. Before sending a team to the practice field every member must know the overall plan, what is expected of them individually, and have a clear vision of what success looks like.

How often should this teaching/training occur? Thomas Watson said, "There is no saturation in education." We agree wholeheartedly. There is no point at which anyone can stop learning. There is no point at which you can or should stop training your salespeople. Even the most seasoned team members can learn from new strategies, technology, research, and successes. Monthly, quarterly, and yearly learning sessions are recommended. Your individual situation will dictate the plan you follow, but we encourage you to include on-going education in your sales plan. As a parallel, you might ask why medical doctors are required to participate in on-going education. Doctors, like all professionals, are required to stay current with the latest developments in their field.

3. **Coach:** To continue our sports metaphor, the coaches will walk the players through the plays so they can learn their positioning and responsibilities on every play. Then, and only then, will there be a few practice plays, first in slow motion and then at full game speed. The teacher may run through several plays showing the player exactly where he is supposed to be during the play and what he is supposed to do. After many repetitions and hours of practice, the coach is ready to put the team on the field. Coaching, after all, is done from the sidelines. Coaches do not actually run the plays, players do.

Before a sales manager can put his team on the field, each member will know what activities lead to success, how much of each kind of activity is required, what boundaries and limits they must be aware of, what resources are available, and where to get them. Fielding a team or starting a game before these items are accomplished will result in unsatisfactory outcomes. Role-playing and video-taping sessions are ideal tools to enhance learning and support a coach's goals.

Another important part of coaching is observing the team from the sidelines, giving encouragement, and making corrections during time-outs. These mid-course corrections can, and do, win games. The effective sales manager sets aside time to review "game film" with every one of his salespeople. This review includes call reports, sales strategy, and tactics. During this review the sales manager will make adjustments for missed plays. For instance, if a salesperson was for one reason or another unable to meet their prospecting activities in the prior week, the sales manager will ask that time gets scheduled in the coming week for this all-important activity.

4. **Motivate:** Have you worked for someone who inspired you to improve your skills, invested time with you, encouraged you to work hard, and allowed you to grow in your position? If so, that person was likely a good motivator. This skill is not easy to master. It can be difficult to maintain especially if sales and revenue are not growing at a quota rate, competition gets more aggressive, and the economy is slowing down.

We should point out that it is during trying times that the sales manager must demonstrate calm and resolve. Any apparent fear or uncertainty during these times can devastate a sales team. There are many ways to cope with failure, but the one we like best for sales managers and salespeople goes like this:

- "I don't think of failure as failure, but rather as an opportunity to learn how not to do it the next time."
- "I don't see failure as failure, but rather as an opportunity to increase my skills."

As Henry Ford said, "Failure is the opportunity to begin again more intelligently." A particularly poignant motivational quote for all managers is by Albert Einstein: "In the middle of difficulty lies opportunity."

Positive encouragement can be a great motivator. I once had a boss who convinced me I was competent and could do anything I wanted in the sales organization. It's no surprise that I accomplished a lot and worked very hard for this person. This leader was a great motivator. His leadership style is an example of the Pygmalion Principle which states that people will do what is expected of them (remember *My Fair Lady*?). Its name is derived from a Greek myth in which a sculptor named Pygmalion sculpted a statue of a woman and fell in love with it. His love was so strong that it transformed the statue into a real woman. It is this transformative effect resulting from expectations which is the basis of the Pygmalion Principle.

It is also known as the self-fulfilling prophecy. Sociology professor Robert Merton popularized it in the 1950's. It is a potent motivational tool for managers. Research has shown that people perform better when someone else believes they will perform better. For managers this means they often get what they expect. As a manager, this is a powerful tool that you can harness to work for you. You can also let it control performance in a negative way. It is your job to set expectations which enhance performance.

Salespeople may not want to perform many routine activities: prospecting, updating the Customer Relationship Management system with the latest account information and activities, making sure order packages are complete, or meeting with key customers where there may be no immediate new business potential. However, motivated employees will gladly perform them. Unmotivated employees will not be so cheerful about doing them.

I worked for a boss who said he wanted all of us to "work smart, work hard, and have fun." The idea that we were supposed to have fun was, to say the least, unusual. "Aren't we supposed to be hard at work all the time?" we would ask? However, this boss planned group activities, such as recognition parties to honor achievement, dinner events with our spouses, beer parties, snow skiing, sailing, baseball games, symphony tickets to name a few, that refreshed us and made us want to work even harder for him.

Finally, economic rewards and incentives are great motivators. There is room in every sales budget for meaningful recognition of sales achievements and victories. Bonuses and commission accelerators (provisions that increase the commission amount) are wonderful motivators. It is best to deliver the reward as close as possible to the time of the success, while the taste of victory is still fresh. Monday morning sales meetings are a good time to offer cash awards for contracts signed the prior week. Salespeople begin to look forward to the meetings and presentations.

General Patton led soldiers who would follow him into battle while they were tired and cold because they were motivated. A motivated sales force can accomplish almost anything.

Chapter 18

Fundamentals of Sales Management (For Entrepreneurs)
Or
"What I always wanted to know about sales management but was *too busy* to ask."
The Seven Keys to Effective Sales Management
(Seven things owners/sales managers must do to effectively manage their sales teams)

By Philip A. Nasser

"The task of the leader is to get his people from where they are to where they have not been."   *--Henry Kissinger*

In this chapter we will explore the seven keys to effective sales management. Whether you are an entrepreneur/owner or a sales manager these basic rules apply to you.

Have you often wondered if you had the best tools to manage your sales force? Or, what the best tools for your industry are? Which tools, for example, give you the best up-to-the-minute picture of your sales team's efforts? Which tools offer the dual benefit of helping the sales force perform more effectively while making the job of sales management more efficient? How do you use the latest customer relationship management and sales force automation systems? How much training should you use?

Before we look at the seven keys to effective sales management, let's look at some of the typical difficulties sales managers face:

- Getting accurate forecasts and, therefore, being unable to predict revenue
- Salespeople not comfortable calling at the highest levels in a company (executive management)
- Salespeople chase deals that are not qualified and then hang on to a deal they are unable to win for too long

- Poor sales performance by the salespeople is always blamed on the company's products
- Pre-sales resources (technical experts, product experts) are not used properly
- Turnover is too high
- Skills learned in training are soon forgotten or simply not used

These are difficulties faced by most sales managers. They are not new. They are solvable. Here's how you might overcome them.

Tightly define the market served and the problems you will help them solve. There is a natural tendency to try to be all things to all people, particularly among new, entrepreneurial companies. Here is a frequent example. A salesperson is working on closing a key customer and, during the sell cycle, the prospect asks for an extension/enhancement to the product that very few other prospects or customers will use. Because of the implied importance of the deal and the need for sales, the request is included in the product. This is not recommended for two reasons: first, as mentioned, very few customers will use the enhancement and, second, making the enhancement uses key resources that could be employed in other strategically important ways. A tight focus on the target market will help you resist temptations to make these kinds of product enhancements.

By tightly defining the market served we mean defining the industry, group, and North American Industry Classification System (NAICS) code(s) for your target market. Who are they? Where are they? What are the key demographics (revenue, number of employees, and financial condition)? Once you have done this, it is time to determine how to identify the target companies by name. Purchase lists from associations, list companies, and other organizations to build your database of suspects.

There is a distinction between total market and available market. To illustrate this, a client asked us to help develop their business plan. One product was being sold into a market that had 20,000 members. On closer inspection, however, there were only 5,000 companies who were of sufficient revenue size to realistically be able to afford the purchase. We ended up building an aggressive growth plan, but it was focused almost exclusively on the smaller 5,000 member segment. The important point for building a sales plan is being able to answer the question, "What is the available market for our products?"

Brainstorm with your marketing department for ideas and programs to generate demand such as webinars, seminars, direct mail, podcasts, newsletters, customer testimonials, alliances, speaking engagements, white papers, community marketing, networking, and trade shows.

Define the "ideal" prospect. Among all the prospects in this tightly defined market, which ones are the best? Which ones are your ideal prospects? Specifically, which of them have the business problems for which your company has a solution? Where is the "sweet spot" inside these prospects? How many of these ideal prospects are there? What characteristics do they have in common? To do effective market planning (revenue expectations, quota setting, product planning, territory assignment), you must know how many prospects meet this requirement.

Armed with an ideal prospect definition, your sales team can start each qualification process with questions to learn how closely the prospect meets the requirements. When they identify such a prospect, they can immediately initiate a sales cycle. If the prospect does not meet the requirements, the salesperson can grade the prospect in the Customer Relationship Management system and move on to the next prospect.

Using the tightly defined market and the definition of the ideal prospect, the marketing team can design demand creation programs that speak directly to the inefficiencies and issues your product or service addresses. The leads from these campaigns will be better qualified than if they were addressed to a larger audience.

Of course, some prospects will not meet the ideal definition. They can still represent good business for the company. The important point is all parties, the salespeople, management, executive management, will know the type and quality of prospects they deal with. The quality of the prospect pipeline increases as adherence to the ideal standard increases.

Use a prospect grading system. As prospects proceed down their buy cycle (typical stages are recognition of their problem, making a decision to do something about it, deciding on criteria for a solution, evaluating alternatives, viewing demonstrations, inviting proposals, checking references), they become better prospects, assuming your company is able to meet their needs. However, to be able to recognize where the prospect is in their buy cycle, you need a prospect grading system.

Simple grading would be A, B, C, and D. For example, to be qualified as a "D" prospect, it may only be necessary for the prospect to be in the target market. An "A" prospect would have to meet many more qualifications, e.g., have seen your solution and agreed that it meets their needs, have the funds budgeted, checked your references, and have shown a preference for your solution. A good grading system can take many forms. You can't manage a sales team or market effectively without one.

Why grade prospects? Grading each prospect in a company's pipeline accomplishes several important things:

- Forces a description of the characteristics/milestones at each level in the pipeline
- Gives everyone a more realistic view of pipeline value: salespeople, sales, and executive management
- Places a dollar value on each stage in your pipeline
- Provides insight for future business
- Improves forecasting accuracy
- Helps marketing determine which prospects are responding to their demand creation efforts

- Identifies key deals that deserve more resources
- Motivates salespeople to perform activities that increase the size and value of the pipeline

Use a sales methodology. A sales methodology is a sales process that works optimally for your company. In another chapter we note that the majority of sales methodologies work well. We point out it isn't important to have the best sales methodology, it is just important to have one that works exceedingly well for your company.

"It's just a question of results. Everyone wants results, but nobody wants to do what it takes to get it done!"
--Clint Eastwood as Dirty Harry, in Sudden Impact

How appropriate for many salespeople running a territory. Absent a goal, directions, and the desire to do what it takes, there is little chance of achieving the desired objective.

If you know where you want to go, you need a map. A sales methodology gives you that map. It will describe the sales behaviors needed at each stage of the prospect's buy cycle. What are the stages a prospect goes through in the process of buying a product/service? The sales methodology adopted will accommodate each of these stages and provide specific recommendations for what the salespeople are to do at each stage.

A typical sales methodology prescribes best-practice sales behaviors for these stages: qualification, needs discovery, funds availability, verification of ability to meet prospect needs, demonstration of capabilities, proper use of references, proposal preparation, and final presentation.

To be most effective, you would customize the methodology to your needs. However, a standard methodology is better than none at all. If everyone in the organization adopts and adheres to the methodology, sales productivity will improve. Document the methodology in writing and train everyone on it. Make it a requirement for new hires.

Conduct sales training with tools from the methodology (e.g., models for qualification phone calls, initial discovery meetings, identifying major inefficiencies in the prospect's operations, staying in sync with the prospect's buying cycle, demonstrations, and proposals).

The real value of a sales methodology lies in the tools developed for the sales team and sales management.

Set salesperson activity expectations. Define in writing the sales activities that are expected of a salesperson. What, how many of each, over what period of time. One document our clients have used is titled a Sales Expectation or charter. It includes all the items from a traditional position description with one important addition: the specific sales activities that are expected of the salespeople. These include expectations for the activities regarding prospects, customers, industry associations, and administrative duties. The document can be used during the interview process to make sure all applicants understand what is expected of them.

If you want to increase sales, increase the key sales activities that lead to sales. This is actually the easiest way to increase sales: find out what the key sales activities are that lead to sales and do more of them. We are talking about the quantity of an activity, not the quality. We recommend clients start with quantity first, followed by efforts to improve quality. As it turns out, the quantity of sales activities are the easiest to improve. They can be installed with a sales force in one week. Work on the quality component takes more management time and effort since there are many more subtleties. It is important to remember that firms will experience an increase in sales productivity when there is an increase in sales activity.

Last, be sure to set quotas for salespeople. You can't manage what you can't measure. Sales quotas are a good management and measurement tool.

Quotas are best if they include a stretch component. Make quotas difficult but attainable. Accelerated quotas with a near-term, mid-term, and long-term component are best. For instance, a system that includes a monthly, quarterly, and annual quota (and incentives/accelerators that are paid periodically) is better than just an annual quota since it provides a chance for success and payment at many points across the fiscal year.

Reward performance. Quotas for salespeople are of fundamental importance. Making sure rewards are tied to quota attainment is even more important. You need a reward for focusing on a goal, working hard to achieve it, and achieving it. Goals without rewards can be de-motivators. They can be seen as goals that only benefit management. That's not good.

What are some examples of effective rewards? While dollar bonuses appear to be the best motivators, other rewards are effective. Among these are formal recognition in front of a group, plaques, trips for the winner and spouse or significant other, gift certificates (for almost anything to almost any store/shopping center), and electronic devices (iPods, DVD players, LCD TV's, Bose systems, or portable digital assistants).

Have fun-Make it fun!! Of course, some people argue that work, by definition, is not fun. We like to say that we can make work fun. Andrew Carnegie said, "There is very little success where there is little laughter." Since we have to do the work, why not make it as fun as possible? This starts with having an honest, supportive environment at work. Assuming that is in place, why not hold frequent all hands meetings/team-building sessions and include on the agenda skits from the various departments? Include business items as part of the meeting as well. The skit topics can be anything company related. It is OK to have fun with other departments, team-members, project leaders, bosses, and executive management.

Other ideas for fun are theme dress days, birthday cakes for employees, intra-departmental athletic contests, and special prizes and recognition for achievements by the company.

Chapter 19

Seven Steps to Recruiting the Best Salespeople

By Philip A. Nasser

"The man who starts out simply with the idea of getting rich won't succeed; you must have a larger ambition."   *--John D. Rockefeller*

Does your company have a first-class salesperson recruiting system?

All other things being equal, a company with a great sales team will outsell one with an average sales team. Imagine if your sales force was comprised of "A" players from top to bottom, with everyone meeting their sales quotas, with low or non-existent turnover! Most people agree that would be fantastic and ideal. Most companies are not in this position. More typically you find a mix of performers who are great, mediocre, poor, and up-and-comers. Still, the goal remains to recruit the best sales force. How do you go about recruiting the best sales team?

Many clients who struggle with building a replicable system that delivers quality results on a consistent basis have asked us this question. In reply we developed a recruiting system/process that greatly improves your chance of attracting the best to your company. This straightforward system includes many of the tools and processes our experience has shown are necessary to achieve excellence in this area.

"Premise: employment decisions based on good, solid information are generally correct. Employment decisions based on "gut feel" are more likely to be wrong."   *--Ron Spencer*

Define the ideal candidate. What does the ideal candidate look like? Be as specific as you can: education, work experience, demonstrated successes, industry knowledge, personality traits, energy, or style. Put it in writing and share it with the hiring team for their feedback and agreement before the interview process begins.

Describe the Position. This document, frequently called the position description, will include the position title, reporting structure, summary of work performed, specific duties, requirements (the "must-haves" for the person in this position), activity expectations (e.g., new prospect phone calls per week, new prospect meetings per week, surveys per month, demonstrations per month, customer meetings per month, and training). Presenting activity expectations early in the interview process is critical to letting the applicant know exactly what is expected.

Several clients have called this document the Salesperson Charter and use it in the pre-hire environment to make sure applicants know exactly what is expected of them. It lets you make a qualifying decision about whether or not the applicant is willing or able to do the required work.

Identify Likely Sources. These may include existing employees, direct recruiting, internet job boards, social networking sites, employment agencies, and recruiting firms. Once sources are identified, assign someone responsibility for generating qualified candidates.

Create a Sales Candidate Model. This is an evaluation tool that lists the job requirements and gives everyone in the company who interviews the candidate the opportunity to grade the candidate on each requirement. This model gives the hiring manager a comparative ranking tool. Since it is so useful, most of our clients have adopted this or a similar model.

"A resume is a person's balance sheet with no liabilities."   *--Robert Half*

Plan Potential Interview Focus Areas. A plan for the interview improves your chances of learning what you want to know and demonstrates respect for the candidate. What are you trying to accomplish during the interview? What questions will you ask to gather the data you need? Potential focus areas are: critical choice points (schools, major job changes), duties and responsibilities, a failure and what was learned from it, measurable accomplishments/performance, relationships with people, likes and dislikes, self-evaluation, career interests/goals, hobbies, and other leisure time pursuits, and missing or incomplete information.

"Asking the right questions takes more skill than giving the right answer."
--Carolyn Byram

Develop a Candidate Interview Questionnaire. We have developed interview tools such as this for clients who are interested in getting feedback on key areas from everyone who interviews the applicant. Based on your requirements, you may develop questions to determine assertiveness, judgment, people orientation, attention to detail, sales cycle management, and stress management.

Check References. If you are under time constraints, there is a tendency to skip this all-important step. Don't do it. While a bad reference is as hard to find as a good employee, vital information can be gathered from a candidate's references or, even better, someone who a reference refers you to. We advocate that there be two phases to the reference check. The first focuses on verifying key information such as education (colleges and universities are happy to verify the degree(s) of their graduates over the phone), employment dates, and employment gaps. If possible, avoid past employer's Human Resource departments. In the second phase we encourage our clients to ask past supervisors, peers, and co-workers eight tough reference checking questions that we supply.

Chapter **20**

The Five Big Incentive Compensation Mistakes That Plague Sales Departments

By James W. Obermayer

If not properly motivated by the prospect of gain with attainable goals, many salespeople never realize their full potential. They wander about making sales in a self-directed manner, driven by their needs and comfort level, regardless of the requirements of the company. The result is that the company has high salespeople turn-over, irritatingly large sales training and recruiting costs, lost market share, and management has to answer that disgusting question, "Why aren't you making forecast?"

While I cover five of the most common errors in sales compensation practices, if the salespeople aren't making quota (30-40%), the quotas are too high and more discouraging than motivating.

I know the president of a very well known company with a great reputation in the Midwest who treated his employees fairly and produced over $500 million a year in sales. However, his salespeople were never happy. Every year the compensation program demanded that each salesperson achieve a 35% growth target. Bonus money did not pay out until the salesperson hit 110% of the growth target.

The company grew 18-20% a year. Wall Street patted the president on the back, but the salespeople's compensation program never paid off because the majority failed to make the 35% number, which reinforced the company president's suspicions. He would say, "See, if I don't set a 35% growth number we'd never get the 20% I promised the Street."

This learned instinctual reaction is similar to a habit which my dog Darby displays. Almost every day someone comes to the front door and drops off a flyer selling something. Every time Darby the Wonder Collie charges the door, fur flying, and barks viciously at the intruder. The intruder drops the flyer and retreats. Darby barks until the person is off the property. She connects her barking and the person leaving. I call it the

Darby Syndrome. Everyday her belief is reinforced because someone comes to the door, she barks, the person most often leaves and she is satisfied. Life is wonderful and the Collie has earned her dinner.

The president was in the same vicious cycle. His belief was reinforced in a negative way once he set an out-of-sight goal and the salespeople hit only 20%. He could never back down even if his salespeople were in pain. Sometimes he paid bonuses anyway which compounded the issue by paying for performance that was never reached. He was afraid that if he set realistic goals, no one would make the number. Meanwhile his sales force was desperately unhappy. They were captured in a small town in the Midwest and turn-over was still above 20%. Few salespeople were satisfied, materially or mentally, even as the company enjoyed glowing reports on Wall Street.

Simply stated, remember that incentive compensation plans operate best when they are an incentive (yes, I really said that). While whole books are written on this subject, the following five tips will solve many of your incentive compensation weaknesses.

1. **Set Realistic Goals.** Never forget, salespeople are employees too. If you need to grow the company 15% next year, set growth targets 5%-8% above what you need. Stretch them, but don't break them. Religiously follow the next four points to make this one work.

2. **Make sure everyone is on the same plan.** Every salesperson (inside or outside), Sales Manager, Regional Manager, VP of Sales, World Wide Sales Manager, Channel Manager, OEM Manager, GSA Salesperson or GSA Sales Manager, or National Accounts Manager, should carry a quota that is similar in nature. See #3.

3. **Monthly and Quarterly Goals.** Every one of the aforementioned sales staff should have a monthly and quarterly sales goal. Only having yearly goals and annual group hugs perpetuates mediocre performance. The goals must be similar for everyone. For example, the sales manager must have the total goal for his six salespeople. They should get paid a bonus if they make the combined number. They should get paid just like the salespeople under the same plan. For instance don't pay the salespeople on volume and the sales manager on profit. Profit could be one of his or her goals but not the whole thing. The manager needs the same pressure and pain that all of the salespeople feel.

4. **Don't make the plan too complicated.** If the salesperson needs a calculator to understand the compensation program, you have a problem. If they can't easily understand the program it is no longer a motivator. Plus, accounting will curse management every month as they try to find their way through the maze of rules and conditions, grandfathered accounts, special incentives, multiple step programs based on volume, and every other convoluted mess

a non-sales manager can devise to supposedly motivate salespeople.

5. **Don't forget. Honor and recognition are the prime motivators.** Once the basic cash needs are met, properly applied honor and recognition will outstrip other incentives. Every award show, trophy, entertainment statue, or military medal is designed to grant extraordinary honor for extraordinary performance. Use it to your advantage. Honor the best in your organization. The best can be:

    -   The highest quota achievement
    -   The most consistent performer (makes quota every month)
    -   The seller of the most balanced product line (makes quota on all products in the line).
    -   All of the above is really your best performer!

The combination of these three traits creates the best salesperson in most organizations. I call it the balanced performer. They are the most valuable person in the company,

Follow these simple guidelines and you will succeed where you have failed in the past. By the way, when your salespeople make quota, sales turnover will drop, sales expenses will decrease, profits will increase, and everyone will be happier.

Chapter 21

Lost Sales: What Can Be Learned From Them? How to Avoid Them?

By Philip A. Nasser

"Defeat should never be a source of discouragement but rather a fresh stimulus."   *--Robert South*

Win Some, Lose Some

The good news is no one individual, project team or company wins all their proposals. Very few win as much as 75% of them. Most of us are in the 25-50% range. That doesn't mean we have to be happy with the situation. It is just a fact. Lost sales do, however, represent a rare opportunity to learn important things about our product or service.

"We liked your proposal, but..." When a prospect starts the discussion this way our spirit sinks. (After all, we only work on deals we know we can win.) We know what is coming next and would rather not hear it. The normal instinct is to want to move on to the next item on your agenda, not to listen to the rejection coming from the prospect, especially if we thought we would win the contract or worse, had forecasted the sale.

If the decision to use another firm is final, though, there's still a wealth of valuable market intelligence buried in that decision. To improve our odds of winning in the future, listen to the message the prospect (market) is giving us.

Just Ask

When a prospect calls to inform us of their decision to go with another proposal, there's one way to find out what we need to know: ask. Our first reaction could be to assume we know why a contract was given to someone else. Resist that temptation. Prepare to turn the situation into a learning opportunity.

Clients, like the rest of us, do not like to deliver bad news. It is difficult and uncomfortable. For these reasons, and possibly to assuage their guilt, they are generally open to answering a few questions. They realize we have invested valuable time and resources in meetings, research, and proposal preparation and understand our desire to learn from the situation.

First, listen for the reasons the client chose another solution. Also ask if you can schedule a short follow-up meeting so you can learn what not to do in the future. Most clients are willing to help and will agree to a meeting. Take a few minutes to absorb the news and then draft a handful of questions that will identify ideas for improvement.

Perception Is Reality

Most deals are lost for one of two reasons. The first has to do with you and it's this: you did not understand the prospect's needs fully and did not present a compelling enough value proposition to cause the prospect to change the way they are doing things now. Possibly you didn't do enough preparation, were superficial in your analysis, didn't talk to the right people in the prospect's organization, or were in a hurry. This heightens the importance of thorough discovery during your meetings with the prospect. Your ability to deliver value, in a manner the prospect wants, depends on your grasp of the prospect's problems and objectives. Even slightly misinterpreting something in the prospect's environment can leave you with a flawed, losing proposal. If, after listening to the reasons the prospect chose another solution, you learn that your firm could have performed the necessary services and satisfied the prospect's needs, you know you need to work on improving your discovery and presentation methods.

The second, more common, reason deals are lost has to do with the prospect's perception of our capabilities. They may not have perceived that we were able to understand their needs and deal with their issues. The prospect's perception was that, for one reason or another, we could not perform or they did not perceive the value in our recommendation. Remember---*their perception is their reality*. This is closely aligned with the first reason deals are lost but is different in a key respect: the most important factor in a deal is what the prospect thinks and believes, their perceptions. It doesn't matter if *we know* we can solve the prospect's problems. It only matters if the *prospect knows* we can solve their problems. Our job is to build the images, concepts, and solutions in the prospect's mind (their perceptions). If, after listening to the reasons the prospect chose another solution, we learn the prospect had a misperception about our capabilities, we need to understand how it happened and make sure it doesn't happen in our next prospect situation.

Important Questions: "Did I Miss Anything?" "Is There Anything Else?"

To avoid the second reason above for lost deals, it is important to review our understanding of the issues with the prospect before we make any conclusions or recommendations. Ask these important questions: did I miss anything? Is there anything else? Encourage the prospect to challenge anything in our summarization. Try to test everything we know about the prospect, including objectives, ideal outcomes, must-haves, timing, and executive sponsorship. We may discover weaknesses in our fact-gathering that we can correct on the spot. We may learn that we correctly diagnosed the problem, but some element in our fact-gathering was off.

Asking these two questions accomplishes several things. The prospect is given a chance to correct or supplement our understanding of any of the facts surrounding their situation. If the prospect believes we have missed one or more important points, this is their opportunity to tell us. When we ask these questions, the prospect knows we are being thorough. It adds to our professionalism and builds confidence in our thoroughness. It can prevent the prospect from, at a later date, saying we forgot to include something because they will remember that we asked the question, "Is there anything else?"

Will you get straight answers?

Maybe. It can be uncomfortable for us and our prospects to sit through a discussion of why one solution was chosen over another. Some prospects will sidestep the issues and get the meeting over with as soon as possible while others will go into more depth. In either case, we're only looking for one or two areas to work on, so it's worth the investment of time, even if some prospects seem reluctant to talk.

We can turn today's loss into tomorrow's win by eliminating guesswork and getting the story straight from the prospect, not from our assumptions or guesses. What we assume is probably much worse than the truth anyway.

Chapter 22

Implementing a Successful Solution Selling System

By Philip A. Nasser

"We must become the change we want to see."   *--Mahatma Gandhi*

Our client had invested in a well-respected sales training program expecting to increase their sales force's productivity and prepare the company for expected growth. At a minimum the client had expected to see an immediate, preferably dramatic, increase in their pipeline, to be more exact, an increase in the number of prospects and in the dollar value of their pipeline. While there had been some sales improvement, the client wasn't sure if it was because of the recently completed training or because of several new products which were just released. Secretly, he worried it was the latter. We were contacted to assess the effectiveness of the implementation of the new sales system.

We discovered that, while the intentions of everyone involved, the sales team and sales management, had been good, the results were not meeting expectations for several reasons. There were key elements missing in their implementation which we will explain below. This client had an experience not very different from those of other firms attempting to improve the effectiveness of their sales force by installing a solution selling system: frustration and disappointment followed by disillusionment. Why was this true? What was missing in the implementation? What went wrong?

Before going further, we should point out that successful implementation of a solution selling system means much more than purchasing software and training the users on it. Our focus in this chapter is on the full set of changes that must occur for the implementation to be a success. They include the operational, cultural, political, and intellectual changes that drive success. Assumed below is that the sales team and management are average or above, open-minded, and sincerely interested in improvement.

There are six key components in the successful implementation of a solution selling system. While some of this may look like hard work, the rewards are enormous. Here is a short review of the six items.

Executive Management Commitment to the Solution Selling Process

This, the most important ingredient in the successful implementation of a solution selling system, is a prerequisite for moving to any of the following steps. It will not be productive to work on any of the other components without support from this important group. Executive management frequently believes they can spend the money on a sales system and then not have to worry about it any more, that their sales problems will disappear. This is not true. Since there will be serious issues and setbacks, any perception at any level in the organization that executive management is not fully behind the implementation will ensure that it is not successful.

Installing a new sales system requires significant change. There will be change in the way a company works with prospects. For example, salespeople will be asked to position themselves differently, qualify differently, handle first meetings with prospects differently, grade prospects differently, and record the results of all these events differently. There is bound to be resistance to the behavioral changes required. It is not unusual to have folks pay lip service to the required changes and continue doing what they have always done. After all, "It has always worked for me, why change it now?" some will say. Until everyone in the organization knows executive management is fully committed to successful implementation, there will be non-compliance resulting in slippage and waste.

See the diagram on the next page. Huthwaite, Inc. published a study in the American Society for Training and Development Journal that showed an 87% drop in skill improvement 30 days after sales training had ended. We believe this occurs for one reason only: there was no firm commitment by executive management to make the new system work. This further underlined the importance of this first component of implementing a successful solution selling system.

Prospect Grading System

As valuable as a new solution selling system might be, it is much less valuable if it doesn't include a prospect grading system. Prospects increase in value as they progress in their purchase cycle assuming you are able to meet their needs with your solution(s). The grading reflects the prospect's value to a company. For example, an "A" prospect would have met more milestones than a "B" or "C" prospect. The grading should be included in a Customer Relationship Management (CRM) system designed to mirror the steps in a sales cycle. Until all prospects in your company's pipeline are graded, it is impossible to get an accurate pipeline value. Once the pipeline is graded, the salesperson and management will get an honest look at the potential in a territory, region, district, and nation.

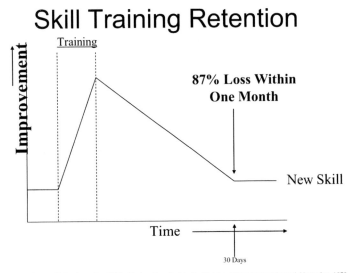

Source: Huthwaite study published in American Society For Training & Development Journal, November, 1979

The goal is to remove the need for sales forecasts from salespeople, sales managers, and regional managers, improve the accuracy of cash flow forecasts and more accurately manage the revenue side of the business. A good prospect grading system can accomplish all of these things. Imagine how happy the salespeople will be when they learn forecasts are no longer required. A salesperson's properly graded pipeline provides the forecast information.

Effective Discovery (Qualification)

Our experience tells us that most salespeople want to do a good job. They are interested in performing well and are willing to work hard to make that happen. We concluded long ago that the salespeople are not the problem in effective discovery. Rather, the problem lies with management and the systems and training they deploy. Effective discovery is dependent upon a clear understanding of how prospects use your company's products or services to make money (e.g., remove inefficiencies, provide better service, squeeze costs out of their operations, and shorten cycles). Otherwise, how would you know what questions to ask to determine if a prospect could take advantage of your product or service? Effective discovery leads to effective qualification, which leads to effective forecasting, which leads to effective revenue and cash planning.

Sending salespeople to client locations to see just how that client has improved their operations is the ideal place for companies to start teaching new salespeople about effective discovery. This is more important than product training. It is here that a salesperson will glean the knowledge of just what an ideal prospect looks like, how to best qualify that prospect and how to help the prospect improve their operations.

Salespeople must have other skills to be effective at discovery: understanding your company's unique value proposition; learning a prospect's vision of a solution; learning how to position themselves as consultants; aligning the prospect's buy cycle with their sales cycle; making certain funds are available; handling objections and learning when and how to demonstrate their solution to name a few. We believe, however, that the most important skill is effective discovery. It is disappointing to see a good sales process lead to mediocre results because the sales team has not been trained well in effective discovery.

Activity Management System

The easiest way to increase sales is to increase sales activity. Said another way, if you want to increase sales, increase those key activities that lead to sales. This is almost completely independent of the selling system employed but, nonetheless, important. There are two components to activity: quantity and quality. We have learned through numerous attempts that you cannot increase the quality of sales activity very much until you increase the quantity of sales activity. You might be thinking, "How could that be? Isn't it possible to increase quality without increasing quantity?" The best answer is it takes repetition to improve quality. Why do pro golfers take hundreds or thousands of practice swings every day? Because they can't make the perfect shot until they have practiced it repeatedly. The same can be said for all sports. Practice makes perfect. The same is true with any sales activity. The more a salesperson practices an activity, the better they will be at it. Increasing the quantity of an activity is much easier to achieve than increasing the quality. In another chapter we will tackle the issues involved in increasing the quality of sales activities.

Increasing the right kind of activities is also important. Suppose yours is a company where experience has shown that no one buys your product until they see it in operation. We would say, therefore, a key sales activity for your company would be a demonstration of the product in operation. Therefore, setting activity expectations for a certain number of demonstrations per month per salesperson would be appropriate. This key activity, and others, should be incorporated into an activity management system and reflected in the solution selling system.

Ideally, CRM systems would provide this information for management, but this generally is not the case. Typically, CRM systems must be customized to accommodate the key activities a company wants to track.

Nevertheless, this work should be done. It has been said, "You can't manage what you can't measure."

Recognition

Since most salespeople are driven by achievement, money, and ego, recognition is a key ingredient in the successful implementation of a solution selling system. Is money alone enough? No. There must be other ingredients in a total compensation program. Recognition can play an important part in the successful implementation of a solution selling system. As we learned in *The One Minute Manager*, "catch them doing something right and compliment them about it."

It is easy to underemphasize the importance of recognition. Imagine if you ran a four-minute mile and no one said anything about it! The average person would be quite disappointed by the lack of recognition. After all, a four-minute mile is something unique and deserving of special mention. There are many forms the recognition can take---awards/plaques, Hall of Fame, stack ranking based on key sales measurements (total revenue, number of new accounts, total gross margin contribution), team competition awards, trips to exotic destinations, and cash bonuses. We have a client who recently took his entire staff and their significant other to a mountain resort for a three-day weekend. It recognized the fine quarter the company had and was something the employees will not forget. While this may be a bit much for key milestone and individual achievements in implementing a solution selling system, you can see how important recognition of this sort can be.

Lastly, make it fun. Work is work, but fun work can be fun.

Regarding a timeline for full implementation, our experience has shown that the time required varies dramatically from company to company and is dependent mostly on the availability and commitment of management.

Chapter 23

Success Equals Profitable Growth

By Patrick McClure

"If you work just for the money, you'll never make it, but if you love what you're doing and you always put the customer first, success will be yours."
--Ray Kroc (1902-1984), founder of McDonald's Corporation

A very simple formula for success as a salesperson is:
S=PG (Success equals Profitable Growth.)
The mission of any business is not just to survive but to thrive. To be healthy and successful requires that the company grow, expand, secure new customers, take on new territories, and develop new products.

However, there is one caveat to the growth equation—it must be profitable. Growth by itself, without profits, is a risky proposition. Growth by acquisition alone can be risky if not balanced by a candid assessment of the potential for profitability. Business basics demand that sound decisions, based on profit potential, be made before hiring new personnel, opening new offices, or moving into new territory.

What, you may ask, does this have to do with selling?

The surest path to effective selling is to understand the business dynamics of your prospective customer. In an earlier chapter, we discussed how you must strive to make your customer successful and the fact that this will push you to success at the same time. However, we didn't define exactly what that meant.

Success in business is profitable growth. If your customer has defined their growth strategy and has carefully determined where, how, when, and why they will be growing, then you are fortunate. When you understand this direction, you can take steps to participate in it. If your customer has not defined their success strategy (profitable growth), then you have the opportunity to help. If you do indeed help your customer achieve greater success, you will likewise achieve it.

Not all businesses, however, measure success this way. Many mature Fortune 500 companies focus their success on controllable growth.

85

Companies such as Coca-Cola, GM, and Proctor & Gamble are market leaders and household names. Their growth strategies are more commonly pegged at a 2-4% revenue increase. Younger companies, such as Yahoo or Google, are not satisfied with less than 20-40% growth rates. If a company is in trouble, they cut back, reduce their employee count, or divest themselves of unprofitable divisions. They may define their success as maintaining their market share and may be satisfied with not losing too much revenue.

Each company you work with will define its success differently. Your job and your success require that you spend time understanding in great detail your target companies' success criteria.

The best salesperson knows how to discover the growth strategy of his target company. Where exactly is this company investing capital? What divisions are hiring and what product lines yield the most revenue? Where is the most activity? Where is the expansion most prevalent? What new markets are being targeted and who is in charge of the effort?

At times, however, you are selling a product or service into a company or division that defines success differently. Perhaps it is trying to maintain market leadership when the aggressive growth patterns of the past have flattened out. Or maybe it is under heavy competitive pressure and is trying to maintain its position without too much loss.

In any event, the correct approach is to develop a deep understanding of your customer's growth strategy because that is where it will invest the bulk of its capital and resources. In the 1980s, companies everywhere invested in computer technology (mainframes and minicomputers) and IT departments were king. Companies that sold these products made fortunes. In the 1990s, the Internet became the new king and companies snapped up products and services which forwarded this technological wave in seconds. Now in the 2000s, the world is filled with wireless, instant messaging, and the convergence of voice and data. Since this is where corporations are looking to grow, this is fertile ground for selling.

Know your target company well and know its growth strategy. Sell where companies are investing their time and money. After all, that's the easiest place to sell and the place where you'll get the best audience.

Your profitable growth is linked to your customer's. Help them grow and be successful and you will follow.

Chapter 24

Why Vacant Territories Hemorrhage New Business!

By James W. Obermayer

Every sales department has a turnover in salespeople. It's accepted with nonchalance by sales managers with hardly a grimace. "Weed the garden," they grumble. "If we don't have turn-over and new blood, we're doing something wrong." An interesting outlook and maybe even justifiably stated if the turnover is in single digits. But if it climbs into double digits, especially over 15%, the cost to the company in training and lost sales is greater than it should be.

For instance, if a sales territory is left without coverage for more than 30 days, there is a substantial productivity loss that's more like a hemorrhage than sales leakage. The typical sales management excuses for not filling a territory immediately are:

- We won't have a training class for another (insert the number of months).
- We have to wait for more territories to open (hemorrhage, hemorrhage), before we can assemble another training class.
- By not filling the territory we can save on their base salary and the person in the next territory can cover it and we'll not lose any sales. (Yeah, I realize it is hard to believe this one).
- We were going to fire this guy anyway so what's the loss? We'll get around to filling the area.

Sales managers I know say that when a territory is vacant, sales drop in half within 30 days. In the next 30 days, sales drop by half again as reps from neighboring areas seek to cherry pick the best opportunities that are left. I think it happens because salespeople are too busy chasing their own opportunities to call on unknown people. Unless the deal is 90%, they will ignore it. In the third month, sales flatten to about 10% to 20% of the area's potential (no one sells these people; they call and beg for the product). The dollars lost in the third month are not a hemorrhage but an outright aneurism. Multiply the number of salespeople you lost in the last twelve months by the number of months it took to fill the territory, times the average productivity per territory. Now you have a feeling for the size of the issue.

Some ideas for bandaging the hemorrhage include:

1. **Create a bull pen.** Put more salespeople into a sales training class than you immediately need and use them in other jobs, as junior salespeople for example, until a new territory opens. The larger the sales force, the more likely you can do this.

2. **Use Recruiters.** I know that for some of you using the word "recruiters" is like swearing in front of your mother. Get over it. Once they begin working for you exclusively, recruiters will more than pay for their $15,000 to $25,000 fee by getting a person into the open area. You could lose $75,000 to $150,000 in sales for every territory that is open for three to six months. If recruiters are working with you consistently, they will always have someone that matches your profile.

3. **Hire a sales trainer.** This person can get people up to speed quickly so you won't have to wait until the next class. For 40+ person sales forces, they are worth their weight in lost quota attainment.

4. **Hire or promote from within a person who wants into sales.** There is often someone who wants to "step-up" and move into sales. It could be someone in technical support, customer service, inside sales, or product management. They still have to be trained, but your risk is lowered by hiring someone who knows you, the company, and the products.

5. **Run smaller sales training classes.** Smaller, agile classes are easy to control. The person learns more and does it faster. Don't wait to train a larger group.

These actions will solve the most hidden and easily ignored forms of Sales Leakage. Don't allow your managers to shrug and say, "It's a cost of doing business." I have seen companies work hard to lower turn-over. When it happened, they quickly filled the open areas and reduced by two to four months the lost productivity in that territory.

Section Five

Training and Coaching

Corporate America has become infected with a deadly virus which results in huge losses of market share and shrinking revenues. No, I'm not talking about poor leadership, although that is a big contributor.

What I'm talking about is a deadly disease called "Massive Naiveté." This is a completely unfounded belief that just about anyone can become a salesman over time. Just recruit people from your office that have the gift of gab, give them some product training and a price book and turn them loose! They'll either make it, or we'll fire them and bring someone else in. Salesmen are expendable. There's no need for training! We'll just hire the best and turn them loose and wait for the results to happen. It's either sink or swim!

The problem is that the organization will be the one to sink. An untrained sales force is the biggest weapon you can give to your competition. Not only are these untrained neophytes losing sales that could have been closed, but they're actively driving away potential sales. An untrained sales team is worse than having no team at all. If members of your primary customer-facing organization (your salespeople) are untrained, what message does this send to the marketplace about the reliability and stability of your company?

We hope you're not suffering from this affliction! If you are, we have some great advice and some good solutions for you.

Modern training systems are modular, interactive, relevant, and effective! There's no need to have people on the street without the sales skills to do their job. Sure, there's never a good time to take your salespeople out of the field and get them trained. There's never adequate budget for training either. But ask yourself this question: Can you really afford NOT to train your valuable sales resources?

This section is devoted to Training and Coaching. We hope you'll enjoy the ideas and solutions we present and will take positive action in your organization.

Chapter 25

Why Should I Demand Customized Solution Selling Training For My Sales Force?

By Philip A. Nasser

"So much of what we call management consists of making it difficult for people to work."   *--Peter Drucker (1909 – 2005)*

I met a gentleman recently who has been a senior sales executive with a Fortune 1000 firm for the last 20 years. He shared this story with me. "I am approached non-stop by companies who say they have the best sales training program for my sales team. Over the years, I have purchased many of these programs hoping to improve the productivity of our sales folks and squeeze additional efficiency out of our work. In almost every case, the outcome disappointed me. Since my results have been less than impressive, I no longer take their calls. I don't trust them to deliver what we need."

When I asked why, in his opinion, the programs were unsuccessful, he said essentially they were too general and did not reflect the situations his sales team encounters in their day to day work. Citing two specifics, he said the training first did not help his salespeople uncover inefficiencies in the prospect's operation because the discovery models were too generalized. Second, the role-playing sessions did not approximate the real-life prospect situations salespeople encounter.

The reaction of this executive mirrors closely what we have heard from executives over the years. Possibly you have been in a situation where sales trainers were brought in to teach you and your sales teams the latest skills and are able to relate to the feeling of disappointment when the training session was completed. The training missed the mark. Why? In this chapter we look at the reasons sales executives should demand that sales training be customized for their sales force so the training will be on the mark.

You might be thinking, "Wait a minute, isn't a little sales training better than nothing?" It is true that conducting a standard out-of-the-box solution selling training session is better than not conducting one at all. No argument there. The popular sales training programs are all good. However, without significant customization, they almost always miss the bulls-eye.

A customized sales training session is the best approach. Here is why.

Sales Methodology

A sales methodology is a series of steps to approach, engage, qualify, and reach mutually-beneficial outcomes with prospects. It covers all that occurs with a prospect (i.e., your defined market) from the time the prospect is identified until there is a happy, referenceable, paying, repeat customer. The methodology builds a value-chain for all activities the sales force engages in during their prospect's buy cycle. While all sales methodologies work, they might not be appropriate for certain companies. Each popular sales training program has an underlying methodology. Is it appropriate for you? We frequently find our clients would benefit from pieces of many selling systems rather than everything that is in any one of them. A customized sales training program is able to take the best of the methodology and incorporate it into a training program that builds a best practice for a company.

Process

Each sales methodology includes or assumes an underlying sales process. Does a company's sales process match the standard program's process? Likely it will not. There are almost always unique features and twists in a company's sales process. When is the best time to start talking about products or services? How much of the process work can be conducted over the phone as opposed to face-to-face? When does the qualification process end? When is the ideal time to use references? Or conduct demonstrations? Or visit a current customer? Each firm has enough uniqueness that standardized programs will fall short.

If a company uses an alternate channel, how does the sales process work for the indirect salespeople? The sales process for direct salespeople is always different from indirect. A customized sales training program should be able to incorporate this uniqueness in a seamless fashion.

Lead/Inquiry Process

Does the standardized sales program provide a closed-loop lead process (lead management system) so a company can be assured no lead goes unserved? Likely not. Who is responsible for qualifying incoming inquiries? The salespeople or someone else? Further, does this work interface seamlessly with the most popular Customer Relationship Management systems? If it doesn't, what is the sense of spending corporate resources to generate leads or create demand?

Marketing departments recognize their responsibility to create demand and generate leads through branding, advertising, direct mail, and public relations. They have been known to lobby ferociously at budget creation time for funds to accomplish this task. Many times they are successful. Does the standardized sales lead process allow the marketing people to track each lead and develop accurate return on investment to justify their spending for demand creation?

Discovery/Major Inefficiencies

Prospects improve their business through the use of a company's products and services. Otherwise they wouldn't buy them. What major inefficiencies does a company's product or service remove from the prospect's operations? What is best practice for discovering prospect inefficiencies? This is the one area where sizeable improvements in efficiency can be made in the sales forces of most companies. Even more improvement can be made if the solution selling system being used incorporates this important requirement. Will the standard solution selling systems accomplish this? Almost certainly not. To accomplish this, the system will need to be a customized sales training program. Actually, unless the sales system is customized in this area, we would suggest not using it.

Qualification

A company's qualification system is central to the successful growth of its sales. Working with misqualified or unqualified prospects is a major waste of corporate resources, but it never shows up on the income statement or balance sheet. It is a hidden cost. As most sales managers will tell you, the skill they most want their salespeople to have is that of qualification. When prospects are qualified well many good things happen. Forecasts become much more accurate, budget planning becomes easier, resources can be deployed where needed, skill-building efforts can be directed to the proper areas and executive management gains confidence in the sales force. When prospects are not well qualified, the wheels fall off.

It is simply mandatory that the selling system a company uses must be customized to its individual needs. Standard selling systems do not meet this requirement and must be customized.

Other areas where a standard solution selling system will fall short are:
- **Scripts and call flow.** These must be customized for your company. There is no by-passing this requirement.
- **Prospect Grading.** Prospect grading must be customized. A standard approach will not be best practice.
- **Ideal Prospect Definition.** This requirement can't be overlooked and is very likely not a part of a standard selling system.
- **Forecasting.** If prospect grading is not accurate and your sales force is not working with ideal prospects, your forecast will be unreliable. Nothing is as frustrating to a CEO as a sales forecast that is unreliable. Inaccurate forecasts are also a key contributor to the short lives of VP's of Sales.

Chapter 26

Shut Up and Listen

By Patrick McClure

"The most important thing in communication is to hear what isn't being said."
--Peter Drucker (1907 - 2005), Economist and author

You are all working way too hard at selling. If you'd stop flapping your mouth for a while and shut up and listen, you would be amazed.

If you're on this planet and you're alive, your absolute priority at all times is to LISTEN. It's hard for me to emphasize this point too much, but I will try.

When a person is speaking to you, what are you thinking about? Are you hearing and thinking about what they just said or is your attention elsewhere? If you're like most people, only part of you is listening. Part of you is not present. Here are the most popular OTHER activities you might engage in while appearing to listen politely to the other person:

- Thinking about what you're going to say when they decide to shut up
- Thinking "get to the point"
- Thinking about why in the world you're stuck listening to this person when there are other much more interesting people in the room
- Thinking about how you can escape being trapped in the conversation
- Thinking about what you should really be doing with your time
- Thinking about past events
- Planning future events and activities
- Wondering WHY they are talking about this subject to you
- Wondering what their real motivation is
- Fantasizing in general

You probably saw yourself on that list. I can assure you that NOT listening to your customer is costing you business. Any classes you may

94

have taken in high school or college on communication dealt with the written word, not the spoken word. Until now, it hasn't been considered too important to actively learn how to listen.

This is one of the most important lessons in effective selling: Learn to Listen.

There are several levels to effective listening. To become proficient you need to function at all of these levels. Let's call this active listening or effective listening. Here are the basic rules of effective listening:

1. Be there, in that time and in that space, with that person.
2. Convey your interest and support. Make it safe for them to communicate with you.
3. Listen and analyze the exact words and nothing more.
4. Don't judge the person.
5. Listen to the other person, not your own thoughts.
6. Don't interrupt. Wait for your turn.
7. Don't get "dumped on." Politely interject an acknowledgment and move on.
8. Listen with empathy. You should be aware of the emotional level of the person you are interacting with.
9. Listen beyond the sounds and the emotion. What else is being communicated? This includes non-verbal signals and body language.
10. What is the person thinking? Can you sense their attitude or decisions? How perceptive can you become?

Do you see what I mean by active listening?

Now, as professional salespeople, you know the importance of connecting with your prospects. What does this mean? It means active listening. You observe, you watch, you perceive their reactions and you listen in on their thoughts. Even though you are speaking, you are also listening to your customer and receiving their feedback.

I once mentored a rookie salesperson who called on a major petrochemical company. This rookie had been trained in all the technical details of his product (a disk drive) and brought along an 84-slide presentation and two very thick books of technical specifications. He was ready to brief the customer on the minutest of details of the product.

During the first 15 minutes of the presentation, a senior manager stood up and asked for the price. The rookie didn't listen to the question and proceeded with his presentation with the caveat that pricing would be covered at the end of the meeting. In another 10 minutes, another manager stood and said: "Son, these look good. I think we'd like to get delivery of 20. When can you have them here?"

The rookie froze and once again did not listen. With a cross voice, he told the manager he'd cover delivery after he'd finished his entire presentation!!

Fortunately, I pulled him aside and got him to shut up and listen to the customer. We ended up taking orders for over 100 of the new disk drives because we listened to the customer! He told us we were done with our meeting and they were ready to proceed with purchasing, and that's what we did.

In my sales experience, I have seen countless sales LOST because the salesperson fell in love with the sound of his own voice and failed to listen to the customer. Don't let that happen to you!

By now I hope I've convinced you of the power of listening and why this amazing ability can change your sales efficiency. What, you may ask, does one listen for? You can't simply listen to every word with the same intensity. What are the most important items to focus on in a selling situation?

Here's a short list of hot topics to be on the alert for:

1. What are the key issues the client has on their mind?
2. What problems are killing productivity in the company?
3. What changes have recently occurred?
4. What is their buying cycle?
5. Who makes decisions and why?
6. How does work get done at "Company X"?
7. If problems aren't fixed, what will happen?

Of course, your questions will be directed to these topics. But if you master the art of listening, you will find that most prospective customers will be more than happy to tell you far more than you will ever need to know about their company. A sympathetic, active, and engaged listener is a prized commodity! People love to talk and for that they need a good listener. Be that listener and you will see a huge positive impact in your life and in your sales ability.

The ideal salesperson is a master at listening!

Chapter 27

Find the Key Individual

By Patrick McClure

"Never let anyone tell you no who doesn't have the power to say yes."
-- Eleanor Roosevelt (1884-1962), U.S. first lady, U.N. diplomat, humanitarian

Besides finding the right company to sell to, the competent salesperson knows the value of finding the right person.

Every sale, in every company, every time is closed with ONE key individual. Think about this. You've spent time presenting your product to various individuals. You've sold, perhaps over and over again, the benefits of your product/service to all of the individuals involved in the decision tree. You've gone through a selection committee. Perhaps you've written a response to an RFP. Then you've delivered an extensive, detailed, comprehensive overview to a review committee, perhaps side-by-side with your competition. Purchasing has reviewed your pricing and contracts and sent the paperwork to the key decision maker for ultimate approval.

Who is that person?

If you don't know the answer, your chances of closing the deal fall dramatically. Chances are your competition knows the answer and has already worked the system. The other competitive team might even have a highly effective salesperson that may have gotten there before you.

Your sales challenge, especially in a large company, is to find out who the decision maker is and find a way to connect with him/her, preferably EARLY in the sales cycle.

The movie *Wall Street* is a perfect example, dramatized Hollywood-style, of how to find the right person and close the deal with them. In the movie, Charlie Sheen (Bud) wants to sell brokerage services and stocks to Michael Douglas (Gordon Gekko), a ruthless multimillionaire who built his fortune by buying and selling companies for a profit.

Hundreds of promising young stockbrokers had tried, and failed, to meet with Gordon Gekko. If Bud could land this account, the commissions on the stock market trading would be astronomical. Many of his associates warned Bud that he was wasting his time, that Gordon Gekko would never agree to see him and that he wouldn't even get past his secretary.

However, Bud succeeded where others failed. Here's how he did it:

1. He researched Gordon Gekko. He knew where he worked, where he lived, personal details about his family, his habits, his clubs, where he dined, who he associated with, his favorite smoke, and his birthday.

2. He regularly visited Gekko's office and befriended the secretary. Using charm, leaving little gifts, and being persistent, he succeeded in gaining her respect by appealing to her personally, not as a business person.

3. He emailed and dropped off information Gekko would value ("warming him up.")

4. Finally he took a bold gamble that worked. He purchased a box of Cuban cigars, which he knew were highly prized and very rare, and personally delivered them to Gordon Gekko's office on his birthday. Because he was now friends with the secretary, he was able to ask for five minutes of Gekko's time. The secretary successfully persuaded Gekko to see Bud.

The same steps may or may not work in your sales situation, but I guarantee that the strategies Bud employed WILL work on any account.

A certain executive who works for your target account is the key decision maker. Find out exactly who that person is. It probably won't be the CEO or President (except if you're selling to a small business). But it will be one or two layers down, probably a vice president or executive vice president. Ask simple questions to quickly learn who makes financial decisions about your product or service.

Before you call on the account, find out all the details you can about this person. The information available on the Internet is voluminous and comprehensive. Use the major search engines (Google, Ask.com, Microsoft, and Yahoo) to search for written references to your key individual. Make initial probing calls into the company and learn what you can about Mr. Big Shot. You will be amazed at what people tell you.

When you call on the company, start as HIGH as possible. The competent salesperson wants to get right to the sale so they want to get as close as possible to the decision maker early. It's much more effective to work from the top down than from the bottom up. Companies arrange themselves in hierarchies with many, many layers designed to shield the key executive from random calls by pushy salespeople.

How do you get to the key individual? If you've done your research correctly, you will have uncovered several opportunities that will shape your strategy. Chances are the key executive belongs to certain associations or fund-raising organizations. They may belong to the symphony or might be a member of a local country club or service club such as Rotary or

Kiwanis. You might find this person sitting on an executive committee in a trade association or industry-oriented executive board.

In short, NETWORK to the key individual. You want five minutes of this important person's time --- away from the office --- where you can state who you are, what your business is, and what benefit you can bring to the table that will help make the decision maker more successful.

You could simply call the secretary and arrange for an appointment, but your chances of success will be slim. Since the executive knows nothing about you, she has no reason to fit you into her busy schedule. Remember, the ideal salesperson wants to accomplish the maximum result in the minimum of time. If the odds of success are slim, you want to improve those odds before you attempt to play the game.

Besides starting high and networking to the key individual, you must meet and befriend other key influencers in a large company. In a smaller company that could mean the owner and his secretary. In a larger company that could mean two or three influencers and their secretaries. In any case, you must never ignore these people or try to brush past them to meet with the "big guy." However, if you have already succeeded in meeting the Big Kahuna on the golf course or over dinner, you've already passed that barrier, haven't you?

I know of an individual who wrote his Masters Degree thesis in business on this exact topic. He claimed that one key to his success while working for a Fortune 500 company was his ability to bond with secretaries. He remembered their birthdays with a greeting card. Occasionally, he'd bring them coffee or a single flower in a vase. He always acted with courtesy and respected their time. He conducted a full-scale PR campaign while he sincerely went out of his way to make their jobs easier. When it came time to get an appointment with a key executive, he always had the secretary's full support. When the boss asked his secretary for an opinion of the visitor, he always got a positive response. The young man became known in the company as a rising young star and achieved many rapid promotions.

The same strategy works well for outsiders with one caveat: Don't leave the impression that you are trying to buy your way into a meeting with excessive and extravagant gifts. Respect gatekeepers and sincerely work to make their jobs easier. Any gatekeeper will recognize the fake smile and the false confidence of a phony immediately.

You must ask two key questions early in the sales process:

Who is responsible for making decisions regarding (your product or service)?

Who does (decision maker) report to?

These will reveal the decision maker as well as isolate who they report to in case that other person is the ultimate approval source.

I have met thousands of salespeople in my career. A vast percentage of the ones who fail do not properly select their target. I'd rather have them spend 80% of their time finding out exactly who they need to meet with than to talk to whoever is available. The executives who can decide to purchase your product/service are usually hard to reach! In fact, if your target is easy to reach, they are probably not the decision maker!

Sales managers should spend time helping their salespeople determine who they should call on. The most successful sales executives are competent at gaining access to executive suites. Less successful salespeople will invariably need training and coaching to master the skills necessary to call high.

Find the key individual!

Chapter **28**

The Value of Value:
How to Sell Anything without Trying

By Patrick McClure

"What is a cynic? A man who knows the price of everything and the value of nothing."   *--Oscar Wilde, Irish dramatist, novelist, & poet (1854 - 1900)*

I'm going to let you in on one of the world's biggest secrets. It is known to only a few select people and has been zealously guarded since the dawn of time. Millions of people have spent their entire lives, without success, pursuing this secret. I guarantee that if you master this simple truth, you'll be able to sell anything the easy way, without effort.

Sell Value, not Product

If you want to sell the OLD way, spend all of your time studying the product, the features, the technical specs, the actual engineering, the MASS of a subject. Then get out there and see how many doors slam in your face. That is hard work and is not the easy way to sell.

The ideal salesperson has mastered the art of selling value. He understands that his customers could care less about the actual product, but mainly care about what's in it for them. They are only concerned with the value of the product to THEM.

Here's an example.

Suppose you need a new car. You want basic reliable transportation so you can commute to and from work. You need good gas mileage, four doors, and good resale value, nothing fancy. The car must have room to seat four or five family members and the interior should be cloth, not expensive leather. You prefer an American manufacturer because cars are generally easier to repair when you can get the parts locally.

You visit car dealers and take test drives. You buy a bright red Chevrolet Corvette that screams down the freeway at 160 MPH, gets eight miles per gallon, seats two people, and is impossible to work on without extensive factory training. It's complicated, faster than any other car on the road, and the opposite of sensible.

However, it is a SEXY muscle car and you feel super driving it.

The salesperson who sold it to you understood what you valued and sold you that, not the car. He realized that you wanted the status, the sex appeal, the flash, the pure joy of driving in such an expensive speedy sports car. He knew that you wanted the image associated with owning a turbocharged muscle car and he appealed to that value.

The sale will probably last only for the drive home. Your wife might have a different value, don't you think?

I once sold an entire office automation system to an oil company executive. It consisted of a minicomputer and 18 terminals all linked together running a very advanced office system (for its day) called All-in-One. It had word processing, file sharing, a spreadsheet, and a calendar.

The company purchased the system for one reason: the calendar feature. The division president had 10 vice presidents. He could never get meetings scheduled because he couldn't access their calendars. When he and his executive assistant found out that my technology would enable him to schedule a meeting, notify the vice presidents, and get instant confirmation that they had read the scheduling memo, the system sold itself.

I could have talked speeds and feeds, MIP's (millions of transactions per second) and megabytes, software and service until I was blue in the face. The executive had a problem and I had the solution. He didn't care that the system was complex, expensive, hard to manage, and a prototype. He wanted it because of one compelling value.

The value of the system (to him) came down to one word: CONTROL.

If you are truly an effective salesperson (or want to be), sell value not product features.

If you have a hazy idea about the value of your product, here's a simple exercise to help clarify it.

Take a large sheet of paper, divide it into three columns, and write the following headings across the top:

Feature (We have)	Benefit (It will)	Value (Which means)

Next to the headings write "We have," "It will," "Which means."

Write a list of products on the left and fill in the other two columns for each product.

In the above office automation example, for instance, you would fill in the columns with the following information:

Feature: (we have) a minicomputer based office automation system with word processing, filing, calendaring, spreadsheet, and email.

Benefit: (it will) allow you to schedule meetings and notify your vice presidents and receive instant confirmation without fail.

Value: (which means) you will be in control and save a lot of time and frustration.

You will find as you work with the spreadsheet that in general, value is expressed in dollar signs. Either you will make money or you will save money. Or you will save time, which converts to money. The simple truth is that people buy products they value because it will save them money or time.

The highly effective salesperson, therefore, doesn't waste much time studying the details of the products he sells. He does, however, become an absolute expert on the value of the product to his customer. This cuts his training time at least 50%, which gives him more time to kick back and enjoy life.

How can you put this to use if you are a non-salesperson?

Let's take a common example from most everyone's life. Let's look at how you would sell your boss on giving you a good raise.

Four words: Sell Value, not Product.

Most senior managers are motivated to increase the market share and the revenue of their business. If they are middle-managers, they might be motivated by increasing the production of units in their division/department. If they are junior-level managers, they might be motivated by surviving the next round of layoffs. The first step is to understand the motivation of the executives because that is a clue to what they value the most!

Once you understand what they value, you translate your accomplishments, skills, and attitudes into words that resonate with the values your boss possesses. If your boss values return-on-investment (ROI), you need to show how your accomplishments contribute to ROI. Your skills directly translate to bottom line results. Your attitudes and your ability to be a team player have a direct impact on the return-on-investment the company has made in you. And you can in turn directly impact the results of your company.

Your "business case" for a raise directly parallels the value of the person you're working to convince. Link your accomplishments in detail to the values espoused by management. Sell value, not product.

Chapter **29**

Your Job in Two Words

By Patrick McClure

"Do or do not, there is no try." --Yoda, Jedi master from the "Star Wars" series

Now that you understand the importance of attitude, it's time to focus on what it takes to become a highly effective salesperson. The first step is to review the exact components of your job.

If you're a salesperson, you can describe your job in two simple words: Close Deals.

Notice I didn't say "close sales" but close deals. Your client/customer wants a DEAL and is always looking for one. Remember the last time your next door neighbor drove his brand new SUV home and bragged to you about what a great deal he got? How about your boss explaining in confidence that he got a great deal on the furniture for the new office? People not only buy deals, they brag about them to everyone else!

Of course, you may have a negative perception of the word "deal." In the past, it has sometimes been associated with sleaziness or underhanded behavior. When you heard the word, you saw images of small town criminals dealing drugs or running a con job on an unwitting rube. However, if you look the word up in a dictionary, you'll see it stands for a business transaction which is favorable.

A popular television show, *Deal or No Deal* glamorizes the thrill of making a deal and involves millions of viewers who share vicariously in the joy of making a good deal or the frustration of making a bad deal. Of course, as a salesperson and a business person, you want to make more good deals than bad ones!

Let's break it down further. What exactly is a good deal? If a customer perceives that you are offering such a terrific bargain that he wants to purchase the product or service RIGHT NOW, then it almost sells itself. That's a good deal!

But what exactly is a terrific bargain? It's the deal that your customer perceives will have huge benefits and value to **him**. It meets a need, real or

104

imagined, that he has. Notice I said it's a need that your customer has, NOT a need you have. The customer does not care about your needs, he cares only about his.

Let's cut to the most basic element in the equation. Who is the customer? Not just anyone walking down the street. It's a qualified buyer with a huge need for the deal that you intend to offer. In short, it is an IDEAL customer.

To close a deal, the sales expert needs the following:
- A terrific bargain
- A great value/benefit that meets a customer's need (not yours)
- An ideal, motivated customer

With those factors in place, the sale is a snap!

You will find the converse of this is also true. If you want to work HARD to close a sale, try the following:

Try to close a sale (not a bargain) with a vague, unknown benefit that fits your need to close a sale to a customer who has no idea who you are or what your company does. That is a recipe for disaster!

I've trained and coached a lot of salespeople during my career. It's astounding how many people don't understand what their job is. The most common confusion is comparing their job to marketing.

Marketing is a critical function in any organization. Companies spend a lot of money to create marketing programs that will contribute to their overall success. Marketing people run advertising programs, build web sites, create brand identity, run PR campaigns, design glossy brochures, and attend trade shows and industry events promoting the company and its products. However, marketing people set the stage and create a favorable environment for salespeople to operate in but are not responsible for closing deals and winning new business. That job belongs to you, the salesperson.

This brings us to the next word in your job description: CLOSE.

Your job is to close deals. Not to explain deals, send out emails, sit in meetings, discuss strategy, visit with everyone in the office, do paperwork, or compile reports. You are paid to CLOSE deals. Of everyone who works for your company, you are the closer. That is a verb, not a noun. That means ACTION.

H. Ross Perot, one of the world's premier salespeople and a terrific closer, said, "Talk is cheap. Words are plentiful. Deeds are precious."

You, the salesperson, get the contract signed. You collect the check. You shake the customer's hand and thank him for the order. You confirm the transaction and collect the purchase order. You handle and complete the exchange.

If you have a deal on the table with the right customer, your job is simple. In many cases, your customer will close himself. If he doesn't, you need to master the art of closing and use it with wisdom. Always remember, the ideal salesperson is a master at putting together a DEAL with the right customer. Although he can spend time handling objections and moving to the close, he'd rather get the job done with a minimum of effort. After all, he has a good book waiting to be read and wants quality loafing time.

If you do not have as your primary role the job of selling, you're probably wondering how this relates to you. What does closing deals have to do with you?

The simplest way to explain this is to understand the importance of completing what you started. Whenever you set out to do something, it is vitally important that you complete it. When you complete the action, you can take your mind off of it and move on to something else. If you don't complete what you started, some part of your mind will continue to think about what you didn't complete. To the extent that your mind is not 100% focused on what you're doing now, you will not be as effective as possible.

You can determine easily if this rule works for you. Think back over the past month or so and consider what projects you took on. It could be reading a book, mowing the lawn, cooking a meal, programming your VCR, learning to play golf, finishing that jigsaw puzzle or anything else. Which of these projects come to mind most easily? Which of them are easiest to recall? You will probably find that the unfinished projects are the ones that most often pop up. They're also the "projects" that you're most likely thinking about on a daily basis. You intend to get back to them and complete them. To the extent that they are not completed, you will continue to think about them.

If you want to have a really GREAT day, write down all of the unfinished actions you can think of from the past week. Then set out to complete as many of them as possible today! I guarantee that by the end of the day you will feel great. You will be mentally alert, filled with a sense of accomplishment, and ready to tackle whatever comes up in the future.

When salespeople close deals, they complete an action. They create a sense of accomplishment. They free their attention to move on to the next deal.

The best salespeople know how to "Take it Easy." They are masters at closing deals quickly and easily. Due to long practice, they have mastered the essential skills necessary to complete transactions and put a willing customer together with a good solution to mutual benefit. Everyone else may play a part in the transaction and everyone else may gain credit in their personal metrics for the deal, but only one person is ultimately responsible, the one who earns the credit or the blame. The salesperson.

Selling with precision requires a clear understanding of your exact role and responsibility.

Two simple words: Close Deals.

Chapter 30

What Your Eight-Year Old Can Teach You about Sales

By Patrick McClure

"Each day comes to me with both hands full of possibilities."
--Helen Keller (1880-1968)

You were born a great salesperson... then life happened.

You grew up and lost the knack. Watch a baby and you'll see a great salesperson. When you were a baby, you were an expert on the art of maximum efficiency. Think back and recall what it's like to be a baby:

- You get to sleep all the time.
- There's always plenty to eat. When you're hungry, Mom is always there to give you some warm milk or some cheerios to munch on.
- Your parents always clean up your mess.
- You're always the center of attention.
- You can get anything with a smile or a "coo-coo."
- You get picked up and held a lot.
- You have no duties, responsibilities or chores.
- You haven't learned to talk so you just listen (less effort).
- You can't walk yet, so you crawl at a leisurely pace.
- Grownups get real upset when you cry. You are always in control!
- What could be simpler?
- How terrible that you've lost your ability to be Easy!

I recently watched a darling little baby girl, my newest niece. I saw a master in action. She's selling herself! She rewards you with a smile. She punishes you with a frown. She handles objections when she doesn't get her way by crying or throwing a tantrum. She can't talk--hasn't yet learned language--so she doesn't respond to your orders. She always gets her way with little effort.

She's a natural born salesperson---and so are you!

An associate of mine shared a classic example of this principle. A sales team was waiting in the lobby of a Fortune 100 company in San Francisco. This was a critical meeting with top-level management in the executive suite. The purpose of the call was to convince the client of the soundness of their (the team's) software design and direction, which would lead to a commitment of several million dollars in revenue. The challenge was to explain a complex software design to non-technical people and get their buy-in to proceed with a pilot project.

There were four members on the sales team: the sales executive, the technical support person, the product manager, and the industry specialist. The first two, an experienced team, had worked together successfully on this particular account and were relaxed and confident. The product manager and the industry specialist carried a large folder with a sheaf of notes, manuals, brochures, and a laptop computer. Both the product manager and the industry specialist were nervous, worried, and concerned. They wanted to review the key messages right then and were frustrated that the account team just wanted to tell jokes and talk about their golf swing.

The team was called in for the presentation. Introductions were made. The product manager stood up and handed out 30 pages of notes to each of the client executives in the room. Then he started his presentation on PowerPoint. Within minutes the managers in the room, confused, asked innumerable questions. The senior vice president closed his briefcase, prepared to leave with a frown on his face. The meeting had turned into a disaster.

At this point, the account team cut short the technical presentation and took over the meeting. "Sorry we're making this too complex, that's our fault," they said. "We didn't really mean to confuse everyone, but I guess we succeeded. (Laughter) It's not really this hard. Let me see if I can take a crack at it." Stripping the issue down to the simplest terms, the technical manager stood up, took chalk in hand, and drew a simple diagram on the board. Clearly and simply, he explained the architecture in terms that a 10-year old child would understand. He saved the meeting and got the order.

What changed? The account team recognized that technical details were bogging the presentation down and the "fun" had gone out of the meeting. No one was enjoying themselves and it was no longer a game. The technical team had lost the ability to take it easy. They were being way too serious and weren't communicating. The account team relieved the tension with humor and then proceeded to lighten the meeting up with drawings and interactivity.

Guess what! That's exactly how your eight-year-old children learn! It is also the most effective method of training. Keep it simple, make it interactive, and have fun.

The next time your account team is planning that important meeting or presentation, keep in mind that if you are having fun, you're probably on the right track. I can't tell you how many planning sessions get bogged down because the team members make the process way too complex. If the presentations you are putting together are lengthy, technical, or complicated, you will lose your customer's attention immediately. If your strategy session takes most of the afternoon and evening, you are undoubtedly complicating it.

Best advice: take a break. Relax. Focus on the simple parts.

Your customers have a need or they wouldn't agree to meet with you. You have a potential solution which they want to hear about. Your job is to show them how your solution meets their needs better than any other option they have considered. It's not that complicated unless you MAKE it complicated.

A child has a talent for going from A to B without making the game difficult. So can you and so can your entire team. Don't let your inherent talent for over complication prevent you from closing deals!

There was a recent movie which demonstrated this principle quite well. In the movie, the central character ("Dave") was a nearly identical twin of the President, who had suffered a near-fatal stroke that incapacitated him. The president's aides persuaded Dave to step into the role of President without telling anyone else so that the government could carry on with minimal disruption. Dave was made up exactly like the president, told how to act and what to say, and even managed to fool the first lady (for a while).

During one memorable scene, Dave found that the government has decided to slash the budget for a needed preschool child care program because there were simply not enough funds. Rather that going to his dozens of budget experts, he turned to a childhood friend. They proceeded to solve the problem with a novel approach. They pored over the budget numbers and found several instances of "fat" in the budget. Then Dave called a meeting of all of his advisors, pointed out the "fat", and asked them if they'd rather spend the money on children than on their pet projects!

This simple approach, bypassing the enormous bureaucracy of the federal government, worked to effectively solve a complex problem. By looking at the problem with a naive childlike approach, Dave was able to solve the problem. He didn't have a preconceived notion that this problem was "unsolvable," so he was able to solve it.

We all have this innate talent buried deep inside us. When you tap into the "child inside of you," you're reaching for the natural salesperson! When we look inside ourselves, we can always find a time that was much simpler. We can find a time where life was easy. We can find the child we once were.

It's not too late! You can still recover your innate childlike talent. It's still there, buried deep inside, just waiting to be set free. Be yourself. Relax, take it easy, take it simple, and remember the joy and innocence you once possessed as a Child!

Chapter **31**

Stop Selling

By Patrick McClure

"Therefore, the ancient sages of natural virtue said:
"I do nothing, and people's contention dissolves by itself.
"I enjoy serenity, and people rectify themselves.
"I make no effort, and people enrich themselves.
"I have no desire, and people return to simplicity."
--Chinese philosopher Lao Tzu (600 B.C.E.)
Tao Te Ching (The integral truth of the Universe)

The quickest way to drive your sales success is to stop selling.

Let me repeat that. The quickest way to accelerate your sales performance is to stop selling.

This perfect sales strategy works every time. Your customers expect you to arrive and begin selling hard to close the deal. They have anticipated your selling strategy and they have lined up all their objections and barriers to moving forward. They know you'll begin pressuring them to sign the contract and close the deal and are already determined to not get sweet talked into signing an order today. They are determined to prevent the sale from occurring.

When you show up, you do nothing. Be pleasant, talk about a few mild subjects, wonder about the weather, talk about your customers' favorite sport or sports team, inquire about their children and quietly listen while they talk. DO NOT TALK about the following:

- Your product/services
- Benefits/value
- Your company
- The deal you have proposed
- The deal you'd like to propose

Be pleasant, bide your time, listen and don't try to sell. You are actively withdrawing from the battle.

110

The customer will be caught off guard when this happens. They were expecting you to do what any salesperson would normally do---sell---and when that doesn't occur they literally will not know what to do. You have created a big void in the transaction. No activity. Silence. Nada.

As we all know, nature abhors a void. Customers do too. What do you suppose will happen next? Inevitably, the customer will bring up the subject and want to talk about whatever topic is on the table. Silence and lack of activity makes people uncomfortable. They will fill the void with any activity. And since they brought up the topic first, it is now fair game for you to proceed with the sales process.

You can see this process demonstrated physically. For example, consider a football game. The players on the scrimmage line move forward aggressively to block their opponents. The players clash, the force vectors are directly opposed. Each player shoves mightily against his opponent and the battle is joined. What happens if one of the players suddenly disengages? Suddenly there are no opposing force vectors, there is only one, and that player immediately prevails. The lack of opposition results in the opposing player rushing to fill the gap. When the opposing force suddenly disappears, the void actively draws in the other player.

Obviously, the process works the same way in any sales call.

Here's another thought to consider. What were you doing in the first place to have the customer be so prepared to do battle? Why has the sales process become adversarial?

Sales done correctly should be a quick and simple process. Any salesperson knows that adversity does not belong in a sales call. It is counterproductive, a waste of time, and extremely inefficient. The ideal sales process, and the ideal sale, is structured so that both of the parties win. If I win and you lose, that is not a good sale. If you win and I lose, that is equally negative. But if both of us win, that is the ideal situation. If both of us achieve our goals, both of us are successful, and no one loses.

How do we achieve this win-win scenario?

The answer is to align the "force vectors" so that you and your customer are always traveling in the same direction and never arrive in opposition. Your intention is roughly the same as the customer. Your direction is in parallel. You are both moving in the same direction at the same time and you share the same goal.

To align yourself with your customer requires research, questioning, and active listening skills. If you know how to listen effectively, if you know your customers, if you "love" your customers, you will understand precisely what they need to become more successful in their job. If you are able to supply what they need, you are moving directly parallel to their needs. In short, you share their "space" and you will both work together to close the deal.

Excellent salespeople rarely if ever try to sell their services or products. They do spend a lot of time searching for people and companies who have a proven need for the services and products they represent. They focus on the buyer and what the buyer needs and wants. They don't spend time overwhelming the prospect with data about the product. They don't hand out stacks of brochures and business cards. They don't present mountains of PowerPoint slides, and they don't try to sell their prospects on a product they don't need.

The reason people have such negative attitudes towards salespeople is because of negative past experiences. They clearly recall when that pushy salesperson forced them to sign on the dotted line when they didn't really need another washer or dryer just yet. They remember being trapped at the car dealership when they couldn't leave the room without signing a contract. They shudder with horror at recalling when the salesperson and the manager doubled up on them and screamed at them to sign up now or forever lose the chance to vacation in this timeshare unit!

All of these negative experiences create negative attitudes. Your prospective customers are waiting for you to exhibit similar behavior! Most clients are on guard, expecting you to try to close the deal. They know you're there to sell them your product or service and their job is to fight hard, to resist, and to win by making you lose.

If that is the selling situation facing you, you have little chance of doing your job or even having an enjoyable time. The situation is already adversarial and the meeting has barely even started!

Recognize that you will have little chance to sell your product so long as your prospective client harbors such ill-will towards the sales process. The solution is to simply do your job without becoming a pushy salesperson.

Using force to achieve a sale may have worked on your client in the past but no longer. There is a much better way and it doesn't require force.

Align your purposes with the purposes of your clients. You are committed to making them successful and they are committed to their success as well. You both have exactly the same purpose and you're both moving in the same direction. No struggles, no force, no contention, no problems.

If you encounter it, defuse any contentiousness or resistance early in the sales cycle. The best way to do this is by asking questions which seek to understand the needs and wants of the prospect. Understand your customer first and understand their past negative experiences with sales. You can even ask them about negative experiences they've had in sales and get them to laugh about them. Tell them your own war stories. Learn to get on their side and work together with them to solve "our problems."

Be brutally honest. If your product or service is not a good fit for your prospects, tell them so, thank them for their time, and move on to the next prospect. However, be prepared for a surprising reversal. When you tell the customer that there is just not a good fit, that they are not qualified, that it simply won't work, many prospective customers take offense. "How dare you tell me I can't use your product? I'll be the judge of that! I want to buy it now, and I want it delivered immediately!"

This isn't reverse psychology. It's just changing directions 180 degrees. When you withdraw from the conversation, it is human nature to reach for the departing person and continue the conversation. Suddenly the deal is back on the table. If that occurs, you will need to revisit the customer's needs because you might have missed one of them. Perhaps there really is a need for your product, especially if the customer insists on continuing the sales process!

The bottom line for effective selling is to communicate clearly, simply, and effectively. Avoid force, pushiness, and manipulation. Let the customer come to you and acquire your product. Don't get in the way of the sale!

This is the essence of consultative selling. It's not me trying to sell a product to you; it's US working together to create an acceptable solution to an articulated business need. There is no opposition because we're both on the same team!

There is another principle related to Stop Selling and that is called the Power of Nothing.

You can accomplish a tremendous amount by doing nothing.

Here are examples taken from the world of sales.

- When you ask a closing question, do nothing until the prospect answers the question. If you do anything or say anything, you will lose.
- When a customer indicates that he is ready to buy, get a signature on the contract. If you do anything else, you may lose the sale. DO NOTHING except complete the transaction.
- Your basic sales process consists of asking the right questions and listening with empathy and attention. DO NOTHING ELSE.
- You can accomplish an entire sale by doing "nothing." Remember the story of how Tom Sawyer got everyone else to do his job? He sold them on how much fun they would have painting the fence. Everyone jumped in to do the job while he did NOTHING.
- Customers hate to be sold. So don't sell, just DO NOTHING while you proceed to make friends and find out more about what makes them tick.
- Opposites attract. The more you reach by overtly trying to sell, the more they will withdraw. However, if you withdraw by doing nothing, they will begin to reach and show interest.

The star salesperson is an expert on Doing Nothing. That's why he is so successful.

Don't believe me? Here's an example taken from one of my clients who recently learned the value of doing nothing.

The client was a highly-educated scientist and medical doctor who was an expert in a very specialized field, working with clients to gain the maximum amount of reimbursement for their medical devices. Thousands of devices and drugs are invented annually. The FDA must approve them and give them reimbursement codes. When the medical procedure is performed or the device is implanted in a patient, the hospital or clinic can apply for reimbursement from Medicare by using this reimbursement code. The way a device is coded can mean the difference between receiving a $10 or a $100 reimbursement. In this industry, what you invent is not as important was what the government will reimburse you for!

Although my client was an expert in his field, he was not an expert in sales or marketing. He felt compelled to describe in technical detail all of the ins and outs of gaining approvals from various government agencies. When given the opportunity to network with potential clients, he would routinely overwhelm them with the difficulty of gaining a reimbursement code. During his presentations, he spoke in technical terms, using medical jargon, and tended to wander from topic to topic. In short, he scared away his potential customers by not learning the value of doing nothing.

To cure this tendency and to teach him the value of doing nothing, we practiced a drill which I call "selling to an eight-year-old." We had this brilliant man reduce his technical complexity to the simplest of terms. Whenever he described a product, we made him use simpler words. As he talked, we worked to reduce complex sentence structures. We practiced over and over until he could easily describe what he did and its value to his customers in less than one minute. Then we recruited eight-year-old children and asked him explain to them what he did. If he could explain the consulting services he delivered in understandable terms to a group of eight-year-old children, he could communicate effectively with anyone.

Prior to this exercise, he was doing a lot of "somethings." After the exercise, he was able to do a lot less and approach the goal of doing nothing. He could simply explain in less than one minute (rather than the previous 10 minutes) exactly what he did and why it was important and valuable to his prospects WITHOUT confusing them or scaring them away.

In short, he accomplished much more by doing less.

This principle of doing nothing has been espoused for thousands of years by a variety of sages. The ancient Chinese philosopher Lao Tzu understood well the concepts of Yin (force of darkness) and Yang (force of light) when he wrote:

"Existence and non-existence give birth to each other.
"Difficult and easy define each other
"Long and short form each other
"High and low make each other distinguishable
"Silence and sound make each other conspicuous
"Front and back connect each other."

Other philosophers and religious leaders from Gautama Buddha to Mahatma Gandhi to Socrates to Jesus Christ have echoed these themes. When they advocated "Know thyself" and the value of silent reflection or meditation, they were persuading all of us to step back, enjoy the silence, relax, and do nothing. The answer seems to be finding yourself in the silence and nothingness.

What does this have to do with the modern world and getting your job done?

The value of doing nothing (or reducing your "doing" as much as possible) is an integral part of your sales process as covered in the above examples. In any sales process, there is great value in silence. A key listening skill involves you being silent and letting your customer talk. He talks and you listen. He is the Yang and you are the Yin. One action defines the other; one action depends on the other. Both of you can't talk at the same time. It destroys the balance of Yin and Yang and nothing gets done. The more you listen, the more the customer talks. The more he listens, the more you talk.

Have you ever noticed that when you are silent, others feel compelled to talk? And vice versa? That is the principle of Yin and Yang applied to conversation. The principle is critical to understanding sales. In order to successfully sell in the most efficient manner, it is easiest to allow the customer to sell himself. This requires listening (silence, nothing) while the customer is talking (action).

If you accelerate this process by asking the correct questions and listening, you will also build empathy and trust with your client. Finally, if you encourage customers to talk about what they need to create success (the prime motivating factor), they will become enthusiastic.

Many salespeople have been taught part of this lesson in their sales training classes, if they were lucky enough to receive training. Otherwise, they learned the lesson the old way, in the school of hard knocks. The lesson was this: "After you ask a closing question, you must remain silent. The first person to speak loses. "

I have personally waited up to five minutes for another person to speak. Of course, I have dozens of times failed to follow my own advice and blurted out another question, therefore failing. It's almost impossible to remain silent for that long, waiting for another person to respond. Try it some time!

By the way, this statement is only partly true. Forget for a moment the topic of win/lose as it applies to sales because that is incorrect. In a good sale, everyone wins and there are no losers. The important part is the silence.

Silence is a "nothing" and it creates a void. If you want to get an answer to your question, ask it, sit back, and wait for the answer. Don't rush to answer your question. Give the client a chance to answer.

If it is a particularly difficult question, it might take the prospect a while to ponder and to respond. Your job is to remain silent, do nothing, and wait expectantly for the answer. If you do anything else, you will distract the prospect from finding their answer and responding.

The Power of Nothing directly relates to your success, in life as well as in salesmanship. The key to success is realizing that the key IS success!

Everyone wants to be successful, no matter whom they are. They may define success differently from you, but everyone wants it. It is the prime motivating factor among all of humanity and perhaps the entire universe. If what you are selling can materially improve your customer's chances of success, then you have a winning deal.

One of best ways to lead your customers to success, and thus ensure your success, is to do nothing!

Chapter **32**

Managing Gatekeepers and Electronic Defense Systems

By Patrick McClure

Let's suppose you have completed your research, you have evaluated your target market, and you have determined that Mr. Big (or Ms. Big) is the *ideal* prospect for your product or service. You have learned everything you can about their company and you have even found out some personal details about your key executive. You understand your own products and you can articulate with clarity your benefits and the value you can potentially bring to Company X. Everything is prepared, all systems are "Go" and you are ready to engage!

You will now encounter your first barrier to the sale, the Gatekeeper. If your executive is in fact the key decision maker, it is inevitable that they will be guarded by a defense system. Just like the moat which protects a castle from being stormed and captured, the gatekeeper represents your first hurdle to cross.

There are two classes of gatekeepers and they require different approaches:

1. **Live Gatekeepers:** The receptionist, the administrative assistant or the personal secretary.

2. **Electronic Gatekeepers:** Voicemail, Spam Filters, specialized email addresses, and customized telephone answering systems.

Live Gatekeepers

The Live Gatekeeper is a person, generally female, who works for the executive you wish to speak with. Part of their job is to guard the executive and to prevent interruptions and intrusions. They have a list of known associates and friends who are routinely granted access to the executive (e.g. family members, the wife, close friends, golfing buddies, and the boss). For anyone else, their instructions are normally to state that "Mr. Executive is in a meeting/unavailable/not in" and to take a message.

The fact that your executive has a live assistant is significant and indicates that they have a senior level position in the company. Lesser executives will normally answer their own phone calls or transfer everything to their voicemail system.

If this is your first call on Company X, your immediate objective will normally be to arrange for an introductory meeting with the key executive. In order to accomplish this, you will almost always need to speak directly with the executive. Bear in mind that the task of gaining an appointment is entirely different from conducting a sales call. In this instance, your job is to convince the executive of the benefit of simply meeting with you. Your purpose in calling is to schedule an appointment, not to sell anything.

The only person who can evaluate whether it makes sense to meet with you is the executive himself, not the assistant. In some rare cases, I have met senior level executive assistants who ARE empowered to decide to make appointments or not, but this is rare. Therefore, you need to gain approval from the Gatekeeper to pass you on to the key executive.

To do this, you need to keep these facts in mind:

1. The Gatekeeper is a valuable member of the Executive's staff.
2. You need to be friendly to the Gatekeeper.
3. A positive attitude is essential.
4. The Gatekeeper needs to become convinced that you have something beneficial to offer their organization, and that their boss would naturally want to hear your message.
5. In short, you have something of value that their boss will want to hear!

In today's business environment, this encounter will almost never be face-to-face. Because of labor costs, it is simply not efficient to have salesmen go door to door seeking appointments. You must operate through intermediate devices, such as the telephone, pager, or email.

Since this initial request, through the gatekeeper, will routinely be over the phone, it is absolutely essential that you SMILE. Genuine friendliness is conveyed over the phone any time you smile. If you're not physically present, at least your friendly voice (backed by a smile) will be present. Be confident and direct, never antagonistic or arrogant.

Your dialogue in this initial call needs to be simple, direct, and friendly:

"Good morning, Mr. _____ please"

> *Response: Is he expecting your call?*
>
> *What is this in regard to?*

"The purpose of my call is to introduce myself to Mr. _____, state my business and arrange an appointment. May I speak with Mr. _____ please?

From here, the Gatekeeper will either put your call through or request additional information. Your response will be something like:

"I'm calling to find out if our company would have any business with Mr. _____. May I speak to Mr. _____ please?"

Again, your call has a good chance of being connected at this point. If not, you may need to supply some additional information. Keep in mind that the administrative assistant normally is not empowered to confirm an appointment on her executive's calendar without his concurrence. Only the executive herself can make that decision. You are only asking for 5-10 minutes to explain to the executive why it is important for him or her to meet with you. You're not trying to sell anything; you just want to schedule an introductory meeting.

In most cases, you will be connected directly to the executive if he is in the office and available.

If you still aren't getting connected, here are some additional tips:

1. Ask for an exact time when the executive will be available, note the time down, and tell the assistant you will call back at that time. When you call back, greet the secretary by name, and ask to speak with the executive.

2. Sometimes, the assistant will want you to send information about your company so they can evaluate whether to meet with you or not. Ask for the email of the executive and send the information directly to him, with a cover note requesting you meet for 10 minutes and you guarantee it will be a valuable meeting (for him). This has an additional benefit in that you will receive the executive's email.

3. Befriend the administrator, make her an ally. Explain why you are committed to meeting with the executive (stress the value to their company) and ask for her help. "What's the best way to get on his calendar?" is a very useful question to ask.

4. Find out the direct phone number to the executive. If you are not getting through, try calling early in the morning or late at night (when the gatekeeper is not screening calls).

5. If you are asked if you'd like to leave a message, it becomes a judgment call. I will generally not leave a message if I've not yet met with the executive. They are extremely busy and will seldom have time to return a phone call from someone they've never met. Would you?

6. If you can't get through, you have no choice but to leave a message. However, always request an email address so you can send information. Many executives will read an email rather than take a phone call.

7. Finally, remember to thank the gatekeeper for their help. Acknowledge with an email thank you, a handwritten note, a card, flowers, perhaps a small gift.

Electronic Gatekeepers

The most common electronic barrier is voicemail answering systems. Some executives have arranged for specialized voicemail systems that they never personally answer but have their secretaries screen their calls that way. Others will listen to messages but rapidly page through all messages deleting anything that doesn't sound familiar. Getting through the voicemail "clutter" is increasingly more difficult.

You will generally call 2-3 times to get the executive directly before giving up and leaving a voicemail message. If you DO leave a voicemail message, here are the rules:

- Keep it short and sweet
- Friendly, positive, attitude delivered with a smile
- Leave a compelling message (why should they call you back)
- Make it interesting, mysterious, intriguing or funny (humor works)

Your chances of getting a return call from your voicemail are about 1 in 20, or 5% of the time, assuming you have left a compelling message and there is a good reason for them to return the call.

If you were referred into the company, use that person's name in the message.

Remember your key objective in leaving a message, and follow these rules:

- Convey credibility
- State your unique value proposition
- Why it's important for them to listen and return your call
- Urgency and convenience

In addition, there are several tactics you can use that may allow you to bypass voicemail:

1. Use email instead. Find out the person's email and request a meeting electronically. You can find their email address over their company web site, from their secretary, by search of Google or Yahoo (type the name in quotes), or via social networking systems such as LinkedIn. Or you can guess.

2. Talk to someone else in the company. Try the marketing department because their job is to interface with the public. They will generally talk to you because you might be a prospect. Ask to be switched over to Mr. Executive, or get his direct line, or get his email.

3. Call the main company switchboard and ask to speak to Mr. ___. Before they connect you, ask for a direct line.

4. Ask who is on Mr. _____'s staff. Get connected to them and follow directions of #2 above.

Navigating the maze of corporate America and reaching your Key Executive requires cultivating many skills, but the foremost is persistence! Sometimes it will take many attempts to actually reach your target, but if you follow these tips your probability of success will dramatically improve.

Chapter 33

Sales Managers Are, Above All Else, Coaches

By James W. Obermayer

The sales manager looked around the room and barked, "All I care about is making quota and bringing the numbers in each month. Now where do each of you stand?" This was the sales meeting.

She was known as a nice person, even a caring person, but she ran her department by the numbers. Her office was located down the hall from the sales floor. The door was always closed and she was on the phone constantly. When a visitor came in she switched to email and sent emails continuously during conversations. Oh, yes, she was a deal maker who made her numbers. Usually. She also had higher than normal sales staff turn-over, did not believe in training, and her sales meetings were status-report meetings.

"I only hire experienced salespeople," she was fond of saying. "Let someone else train them before they get here. When they work for me it's the numbers that count and they ought to know how to get them. I don't coddle them. If they need too much attention, I hired the wrong person."

One day after she repeated this favorite phrase, I asked her, "Jane, you played soccer when you were in high school and college, didn't you?"

"Yes," she replied with a broad smile. "I was never great, but I was competitive, had stamina and could stay in the game and some even said I should consider trying out for the pros."

"How good were your coaches?" I asked her. "Did your coaches help a lot or did you just learn to play on your own?"

She was into a subject she enjoyed. The very memory of playing made her smile. Her coaches, she said, were everything to her. Some were still friends even though many years had passed. They taught her how to be more mobile and agile on the field. How to tackle, save, and even shoulder charge, depending on the position she played.

How long had you played, I asked her? She said that she started young, way before high school, and played all the way through college. Did you

121

need a coach in your later years in high school and college, I asked? At this point she realized my questions weren't as casual as they appeared and that her answers were going to come back to haunt her. But she answered anyway, "I had coaches all the way through and I never stopped learning."

I stopped asking increasingly leading questions when she smiled. "Ok," she said, "I get your point. You want me to coach these salespeople. But Jim, I am not a people person." Pain showed in her expression when she said it. "They need so much," she said, "and I don't know where to start so I don't start. They come to me to make deals and that's what I do. I am a deal maker, not a coach."

As we discussed the issues of higher than normal turn-over, high base salaries for experienced salespeople, and the issues with getting people trained by others in processes that were not what the company wanted, she started to understand.

In time, during our own coaching sessions, she came to understand that she was the head coach of her own soccer team. No matter how experienced they were, she had to work with them, help to them to constantly improve their skills, encourage, cheer them on, and help them be the best. No great player, she eventually said, ever stops being coached.

So we came up with a plan to test the sales skill level of her salespeople and the other sales managers. Her office was moved, the door was now open, the office rearranged so when she spoke to someone she was not facing her computer and tempted to multi-task. She scheduled weekly coaching sessions with each of her direct reports. Her library of sales training aids grew. She settled on one methodology for training her reps to sell the company products in their marketplace. Her turn-over of salespeople went down and making the numbers became easier. She was enjoying watching her people get better.

Jane in this instance is a composite of many sales managers I have met. Don't feel cheated. The story is as real as it gets. She is the John, Joe, and Sue of sales management. She is the sales manager on the floor of the sales center, the regional sales manager, the international sales manager, and the VP of sales all combined. All of them need a coaching philosophy. They need a process for evaluating talent and molding it into the best the person can be in their particular sales position. Are you a coach or is your door closed, leaving everyone on their own?

Sales coaching skills are rarely considered the foremost talent when senior management looks for a great sales manager. Management looks for people who can set realistic goals and achieve the forecast. They look for industry experience. But they should also be looking for a person who understands the value of coaching.

Section Six

Marketing

For years, marketing and sales have fought each other like cats and dogs. The turf wars between these two departments have raged for years in organizations across the land. The struggle for resources, the positioning for supremacy and the quest for visibility severely distract executive management teams across the land.

Good news has arrived! Marketing no longer needs to battle with sales. The war ended in a draw long ago.

Marketing needs sales to survive and vice versa. Today's selling organization considers marketing an integral part of their lead generation engine. Marketing has a huge range of tools available, including a massive boost from the Internet, to deliver carloads of qualified leads to a hungry organization.

If you're not tracking the results of your marketing programs, you're missing the boat. And if you're not integrating your planning processes with marketing resources, you're going to be left in the dust.

Reaching people today and delivering a quality message requires specialized knowledge and skills. The Internet has changed everything. In turn the Internet has changed. What used to suffice as a web site was simply putting your corporate brochure online with a telephone number and email address. Today, savvy marketers are creating corporate web portals and storefronts that attract millions of online customers and generate an increasing share of bottom line revenues. The Internet has grown up. Did you grow with it?

Our next section explores Marketing for the 21st Century. You'll find it packed with our greatest marketing tips, tricks, and strategies. Enjoy!

Chapter 34

Micro Targeting - a 21st Century Approach to Marketing

By Judy Key Johnson

Lexus and Mercedes ads are all over network TV, priced at $100,000 and more a minute, but how many potential Lexus and Mercedes buyers are actually watching each ad?

The daily newspaper has entire sections of car ads, yet most of us aren't in the car market right now and we discard the car ads without looking at them.

As a long-term branding investment, such advertising may be justified. However, in terms of generating immediate sales, mass advertising is far less effective. It's safe to say that far less than 1% of the viewers are near-term prospects for a new Lexus or Mercedes.

From a pure efficiency perspective, mass advertising is an expensive failure. Its *so* 20th century.

A 21st Century Strategy

Micro-targeting is a marketing strategy that has achieved prominence in this decade as a replacement for mass marketing. It is especially effective in generating interest and in sales conversion.

Micro-targeting is defining small subsets of potential buyers with common receptiveness to a sales message. Often a micro-target group has common demographic elements. More importantly, it has common value systems and buying behavior.

It challenges the basic premise of the last 50 years, which is to establish a single, strong brand identity and broadcast it in the biggest forums your advertising budget can support.

Instead of big spend advertising, more companies are crafting smaller messages targeted to specific buyer segments and placing them in more micro-target-friendly forums as PR, pay per click and search engine optimization, blogs, events, and direct mail. Here are two examples:

125

- A 2006 study commissioned by Essence Communications, publisher of Essence magazine, revealed six definable micro-demographics within a larger demographic of black women. The women shared common gender, ethnicity, and age range, but the defined segments varied broadly. The study was made available to magazine advertisers to help them generate a higher rate of return from their ads.
- Another micro-targeting research project undertaken for a New York City mayoral campaign conducted extensive market research and identified similar response to an anti-crime message among both middle-aged white Catholics in Tottenville in Staten Island and senior black homeowners in Saint Albans in Queens. The candidate increased his winning percentage in both neighborhoods.

Search engine marketing – an early frontier for micro-targeting

Search engine marketing (SEM) is one of the first venues for micro-targeting because often demographic information is known through a registration process or segments can be targeted through the use of search terms common to each segment. Although billions of people use search engines, ultimately each search comes down to a single person typing a phrase into a search engine. Because searches are initiated by the potential buyer rather than by the advertiser, the sale conversion rate is inherently higher because of the interest expressed by the Web searcher through the act of doing the search.

One of the most precise forums for micro-targeting is based on emerging technology in pay-per-click advertising. It will allow buyers to adjust their click bid based on age and gender and on the conversion of the defined segments. With information on the conversion rates of different demographic profiles, PPC messages can be exceedingly personal, and, as the marketing expression goes, relevance drives results.

Knowing your target segments

The key, of course, is to know your target segments. What are their expectations? What do they value? Which set of messages is likely to drive the desired behavior? Market research, whether rigorously developed by a professional firm or based on the experience of the sales team with guidance from the marketing department, is even more important when the goal is to deliver high conversion rates based on crafting messages that, to a greater extent than ever before, are personalized to the individual.

A message for every audience

Consumers today create their own personalized environment, impossible just ten years ago. Netflix allows movie fans to create their own individual film festival, at the time and schedule that suits them best. TiVo and DVR threw "Must-See Tuesday Night TV" into the junkyard of the old world, replacing it with what is in essence "My Own TV Network," with only the programs I want to watch, available whenever I want to see them.

With the expectation of personalization, and irrefutable evidence that the more personally targeted the message the higher the conversion rate, marketers will need to spend more time developing and testing the messages. Marketing budgets will shift, with possibly less expense in big budget media but more resources invested in creating, testing, and refining many more messages, advertisements and PR copy.

Micro-targeting is an inevitable marketing force, a result of technological advances that allow individuals to create their own environment, and trains them to expect to be treated as individuals. Companies that embrace this trend early will spend their marketing resources more effectively than their big bang competitors.

Chapter **35**

Is your Customer Named Joe?

By Judy Key Johnson

The Use of Personas throughout the Company

If you have a perverse sense of humor, you could easily play a variation of the old telephone party game where a message is rapidly whispered from person to person. The message received by the last recipient generally bears only a faint resemblance to the original message.

In the corporate variation of the telephone game, you would ask individuals from product marketing, customer support, sales, and development, "Describe the target customer for our product?" Marketing might well respond with a well documented spreadsheet or bulleted list, with Department of Labor Statistics demographic codes and a list of prioritized requirements. Customer support would probably talk about the complainers who call, sales would feed back the people who are buying the product today, and development would be heavily influenced by the few customer calls they were allowed to make.

There's a much better way, which has gained a lot of acceptance where product marketing departments keep up with best practices. This is the use of personas, a personalized description complete with a name and imagined personal traits and history.

The use of personas increases the focus on the most desired customers, improves cross-functional communication, accelerates the requirements process, empowers development to make better decisions, and clarifies marketing messages.

Without personas, each company function has its own imagined target customer reflecting its experience base and means of processing information. Product marketing ostensibly defines customers. However, developers, support personnel, and marketers often have trouble relating to marketing's SIC codes and spreadsheets and fall back on their own experience of what the target customer looks like.

Because they lack a shared vision of the target customer, each function uses their individual interpretation to define the customers, resulting in a disconnect when the developed product fails to match the marketed product and the product the sales team is selling. These differences are generally not dramatic, but with each degree of separation from a common vision inefficiencies enter the overall corporate process and frustrations arise between departments.

What is a persona?

A persona is an invented, highly detailed representation of a target user. Each persona represents a class of real users. Rather than being expressed as a series of demographic descriptors, the user is described as if it were a single real person, Joe. Joe is given a name - Joe. There is a photograph or avatar showing what Joe looks like, he is given an age, hobbies, education, occupation or student status, an income, and life goals. Then Joe is described in terms of his reasons for using the product, his want and need for the product within a real life context, his support needs, and his level of competency.

There can be more than one persona. Joe could be the **primary persona.** In addition, there could be a **secondary persona**, Lee, who represents another target user. This user's needs for the product are considered so long as they do not compromise the primary persona's needs.

Product marketing may also introduce other personas such as the buyer persona. The benefit remains the same. These individuals are so well described that people in each organization understand the user intuitively. They can draw well-reasoned conclusions about other needs these individuals have based on the primary persona description, much as you can intuit a friend's political party, even if you have never talked politics, because you know so much about your friend's values.

The persona methodology is taught in Agile and Rational Marketing Training.

Chapter 36

Expanding Your Product Set Incrementally

By Judy Key Johnson

As a business principal, you may not be familiar with the most important groundbreaking concepts in product management. Yet each of these can have significant impact on the long-term success of your business. Here's my list of the five must-know product marketing strategies for business owners:

1. Crossing the chasm
2. The tipping point
3. Second-mover advantage ("Fast Second")
4. The world is flat
5. The product expansion quadrant

The first four are all books by noted business strategists. They are all interesting and important reading and are valuable for developing strategic skills.

However, in my view, the single most important and timeless concept in product management is the product expansion quadrant.

Every product manager, upon hearing the two words "product expansion quadrant," can immediately sketch this diagram:

Product Expansion Quadrant		
Market Expansion	3 Same product New market	4 New product New customer/market
	1 Same product Same market	2 New product Same market
	Product Expansion ->	

1. Increase market share

Selling your current product or service within the same market is the traditional path for the expansion of a company.

- Your product has been validated to meet the needs of the market.
- Your sales and marketing team knows the pain points and language of the market, which results in a shorter sell cycle and higher conversion rate.
- Reference selling is most effective within a single industry. If you have developed a strong business relationship with a well-known company in an industry, it will open doors for cold calls and shorten the sell cycle to prospects who know and respect that referring customer of yours.
- Marketing promotion costs have a high fixed cost component within a single market, especially with b2b products. Brand building activities such as advertising, trade shows and PR are generally expensed by industry segment.
- Your business and product development processes have some degree of maturity, resulting in cost efficiency and potentially higher profits.
- As you sell more goods of the same or a similar type, your cost per unit decreases.
- The highest profits belong to the leader in a market, who can command a premium for their products. By staying within a market and increasing market share, you are better positioned for market leadership.

2. Increase your share of customer spending

Your customers love your products or services. Your brand has a solid reputation within an industry. Your sales channel has existing relationships with buyers. You have solidified your Quadrant 1 position by steadily increasing market share.

Now you're ready for Quadrant Two, increasing your share of customer spending.

It's a solid business strategy to look for company growth by selling something new to your current customers or others in the same market. Here are some possibilities:

- Add an enhanced version of your current product and offer it as an up sell to your current customers. Some companies prefer to buy top-of-the-line, with the resulting quality and lack of hassles. Typically these enhanced versions can be sold at high margins, bring a positive impact to both net revenue and margin.
- Are you giving away services you could be selling? For example, your product installation team may have gained valuable knowledge surrounding but outside of the scope of their

assignment with your product. Perhaps you can offer billable consulting services.

- Are your partners getting revenue you could be getting? It's traditional for small companies to focus on a narrow product area and bring in partners such as professional services firms or complementary hardware partners. As you initially develop a partnership strategy in order to deliver a whole product solution, you should decide whether you plan to replace those partners at some future time, so that you can position partner contracts and personnel training for this future event. You should be forewarned, though, that partners are suspicious of losing their niche and will often establish direct customer relationships and even encroach on your territory in the future.

- Clients are often looking for a one-stop shop. Ask your clients what other services they would like for you to provide.

3. Making the move to a new market

Quadrant Three is often tempting to entrepreneurs enthused about finding new markets for their products and services. "What an easy way to make more money from my product investment!"

Success in a new market is a significant step in increasing the value of your company and reaching a stable financial position. However, be forewarned, entering a new market takes more time and money than you may plan for.

Business-to-Business products rarely are completely portable from one industry to the next, requiring investment and time to modify the product. If the industry is unfamiliar to you, the product capabilities required for a Whole Product Solution may not be evident until your product is introduced and does not sell as well as projected. Even worse, you may enjoy initial strong sales but find user satisfaction to be low, resulting in poor word-of-mouth, high support costs and product re-engineering.

The move to Quadrant Three requires substantive marketing costs because your company and its products are new to this market. Brand awareness needs to be developed and a new sales pipeline established. The sell cycle is generally longer when you are new to a market and you often have to compete more aggressively on price when you do not have an established reputation to drive demand.

The move to a new market is a significant and exciting time for your company and its employees. By being aware of the elements of a successful launch into Quadrant Four, you will indeed take your company to the next level.

4. The final frontier – new products and new markets

As your business matures, you may decide that your business plan requires expansion of both products and markets. If you have been expanding incrementally in Quadrants Two and Three, you have learned how to efficiently and successfully develop products and services and also how to penetrate new markets. Quadrant Four requires execution of both.

In mastering both a successful launch of new products into new markets and in profitably selling and gaining customer enthusiasm for your products and services, your company has demonstrated capabilities that will serve your continued growth.

Summary

By analyzing your company's position and growth plans in terms of the Product Expansion Quadrant and through awareness of the critical success factors of each quadrant, you are well positioned to make informed decisions about your company's future.

Chapter 37

Plan to Sell Your Business in the Next Five Years?

By Judy Key Johnson

Owning and running a business is hard work. Many business owners expect that as a reward they will receive a large sum of money when they sell their business sometime in the future. They work tens of thousands of hours with no more planning than the thought that "someday I'll sell my business."

The result is a sale price that may be half or less than what they could have received if they had developed and followed a business sale plan five to ten years earlier.

Jim Mitchell (a real person, but fictitious name) is an excellent example of what a business owner should do. Jim is 45 and has owned a medical equipment sales company for the past eight years. His company sells blood testing equipment from four manufacturers. He has five employees, and has enjoyed top line growth of 5% to 10% every year. Jim is the company's top salesman. He has a second salesman, an office manager, and two service employees who do a good job of maintaining the equipment that the company sells. Jim's personal income has grown to over $200,000 a year.

A savvy business person, Jim took a step back from his 60-hour weeks and asked himself, "How much money could I sell my business for if I want to retire in 10 years?" He didn't know the answer, so he brought in a business valuation consultant for a strategic planning session, and these are the steps the consultant led him through:

1. **List the industry categories of buyers who might purchase your business.**
    a. His current industry segments (blood chemistry equipment)
    b. Related but not identical industry sectors (medical office equipment, standalone medical laboratory equipment)

    c.   Industry segments that sell to the same buyers but not with the same products or services (test lab supplies)

The consultant started by drawing Jim's small sales niche on a whiteboard. Then they talked about related industry segments and industries, drawing wider and wider circles of related segments on the whiteboard. Jim grew very excited about the opportunities for business expansion that capitalized on his current sales relationships and industry knowledge.

"I can sell other products to my same customers. That sounds pretty easy if I can work out the rep agreements with the OEMs. This will help me raise my gross earnings, which means I'll make more money now and have a larger revenue base when I eventually sell. It also helps me hedge my bets by broadening my product line.

"Also, with my knowledge of blood chemistry equipment, it would be pretty easy to learn about other types of equipment that my OEMs manufacture. I already have good relationships with them; I bet they would help me get started with some new clients."

Already, with Step 1, Jim has identified several natural areas of business expansion that will provide near-term financial benefits and increase the company's long-term value.

This type of expansion also increases long-term business valuation. Investors' value diversification of business risk so that it is not concentrated in a few large clients or in a single market that could be disrupted.

2. **Identify the types of businesses associated with each segment.**
    a.   Manufacturers
    b.   Equipment sales firms
    c.   Equipment maintenance firms
    d.   Related supplies and services

Jim's business provided his clients with scheduled maintenance and emergency repair for the blood chemistry equipment that he sold them. In this exercise, Jim was asked to identify the core competencies of his company and to look for opportunities surrounding those competencies.

Going to the whiteboard again, under guided questioning from the consultant, Jim said he often won new accounts because the clients had been dissatisfied with the quality of the equipment service of their previous supplier. Jim prided himself on having more experienced service personnel than his competitors, and he provided a 24/7 emergency service. Jim said he had excellent contacts with blood equipment service personnel throughout California and the Southwest. Jim was also aware that one of his OEMs was considering exiting the servicing of their own equipment.

As Jim talked, he realized how attractive it would be to expand the maintenance part of his business. He could see a number of opportunities identified on the whiteboard.

The consultant pointed out to him that the recurring revenue of a maintenance business brings a higher multiple than a business that is primarily sales. Service also generally brings in a higher margin than sales of a commodity product. Finally, investors are often skeptical of the sustainability of sales when the owner is the primary salesperson, leading to a low valuation. On the other hand, a maintenance business is viewed as sustainable even in the absence of an owner-operator.

3. Identify specific companies that are future potential buyers.

Using the matrix of industries and services identified in Steps 1 and 2, fill in company names in each category. These companies, some of whom may be competitors, are potential partners or may be interested in acquiring your business in the future.

By listing individual companies by name rather than keeping your analysis at the industry level, you are identifying future acquiring parties and also potential business partners. As you fill out the chart, you will see holes in your knowledge of the key players. You now have an action item: to learn more about these potential buyers.

As Jim worked through this step, already enthused by the opportunity to expand his maintenance business, he identified three companies that he thought might subcontract maintenance workers to him, and two sales rep companies that might recommend his maintenance service.

4. Compare your company to your competitors.

Your business may provide you with a good livelihood, but that doesn't mean it will be attractive to investors. Potential buyers will value you relative to your competitors.

You may think a 10% annual revenue growth is good, but it's not if the industry is growing at 15%. Although you are unlikely to know the numbers for many of your privately held competitors, look for industry-wide statistics from your trade association.

You need to be aware of the industry numbers far enough in advance of offering your business for sale so that you can demonstrate a track record of beating the industry average. An industry leader commands a premium at buyout time; a laggard will get little interest.

5. Cash flow is a critical component in determining valuation.

Many business owners manage their companies to minimize taxes as opposed to maximizing the cash flow to the owner. This can have negative consequences when it's time to sell your business, since valuation is heavily weighted on cash flow or EBITDA. Investors look for a multiple-year track record of both profits and cash; that's why they are buying the company.

6. Maintain clear and clean business records.

When potential buyers inspect your company records, will they find clear financial statements in generally accepted accounting conventions and legal documents that are complete, protect your business interests, and meet mandated deadlines?

Business sales always involve close inspection of company records. If your records appear sloppy, incomplete, or, worse yet, suspicious, the offering price will plummet if an offer is even extended. With good record-keeping, an off-year for your business may be positioned as an exception in an otherwise strong string of business performance.

Nothing can kill a deal faster than poor business records.

7. Documented, repeatable business processes increase valuation.

Jim took one final step in his self-help program to strategically plan for the sale of his business: He started documenting his business processes. Taking the processes one at a time, Jim and his employees spent a half day at a time documenting different elements of the business.

This activity, which took six months to complete, helped them discover new ways to run the business more efficiently and provided a training guide for new personnel as the business expanded from his growth initiatives.

When it comes time to sell his business, Jim will be able to demonstrate that he is transferring a viable operation that can sustain its achievements without his daily supervision.

One year later

The whiteboard strategy sessions provided the impetus that Jim wanted. He decided to focus on expanding his service business beyond his sales territory through a mix of remote personnel and subcontractors using business procedures that meet Jim's quality standards.

His biggest coup was persuading a major equipment manufacturer to hand over its nationwide equipment service business to his company region by region over a one-year period. This expansion is going well. Margins are better than in equipment sales and the revenue will exceed that from equipment sales within two years at the current growth rate.

Jim also decided to pay more attention to the paperwork side of his business, creating records not just for his own requirements but with awareness that they will be examined by a future buyer.

Five years later

Five years haven't yet passed, but Jim is now prepared for the day when he's ready to sell his business. He'll have a nationwide medical laboratory equipment service business and continue to expand his equipment sales territory. His business records will pass due diligence tests and business operations will be based on standard operating procedures. Cash flow and profitability will be well above the industry average.

Jim's business is a success, a desirable acquisition for investors. Let the bidding begin.

Chapter **38**

How to Create a Tactical Marketing Plan in Two days!

By James W. Obermayer

How many times have you heard the old saw, "If you keep doing what you've been doing, you'll keep getting what you've got." This is especially true in marketing. From year to year, so many companies just repeat last year's marketing programs. Does that make sense?

2500 years ago Heraclitus said, "You can't step in the same river twice." The river in your case is the marketplace. What you did last year for last year's products will not necessarily work for this year's customers.

Your strengths and weaknesses have changed. The opportunities and threats have most likely grown with economic changes and new competitors. The only way I know to be sure that the money you spend on marketing this year (2-20% of this year's revenue) will not be wasted is to create a new marketing plan every year.

Every good plan has a strengths, weaknesses, opportunities and threats (SWOT) situation analysis. From the SWOT flow goals, objectives, strategies and tactics. Without going through this thought process, which allocates money and labor based on the potential for the highest possible return, money and talent will most probably be wasted. What a shame.

Casey Stengel said it best (maybe better than Heraclitus) when he told an assembled group, "If you don't know where you're going, you'll end up someplace else." Someplace else for so many is behind their competitors, not a real pleasing position (ask the number two dog behind the lead sled dog).

The way to solve this is to insist that a tactical marketing plan be created for your company. You can do this in two days. The recipe is:
1. Create the SWOT. Assemble the stake holders. Titles in attendance include: marketing and sales management, all agencies that service marketing, customer service, even finance and manufacturing (they should know what's gong on in the marketplace).

2. Get the assembled group to list the SWOT Strengths, Weaknesses, Opportunities and Threats facing the company.

3. Because you will have many items in each category of the SWOT, you will ask the group to choose the most important items in the SWOT because these issues are the basis for the Objectives, Strategies and Tactics. The plan should only be created from the top issues identified in the SWOT.

4. Now that the SWOT is prioritized, you can create objectives for the year, the strategies to achieve the objectives, and the tactics to complete the strategies. There may be a dozen or so objectives, two to three times as many strategies, and many, many tactics.

Creating a plan takes about two days for an average company, less for smaller single product companies. I have hosted dozens of these planning sessions and always found that the participants leave with great insight and plans of action to win in the marketplace. When the two days are done the only items that have to be completed are budget, spreadsheets for events and media programs, and schedules for direct mail launches. Marketing management completes these supporting documents. If the budget is too big, you go through the plan and delete the tactics that are the most costly with the least opportunity for a measurable return on investment.

Your end result will be tactics that are budgeted, have a time frame for completion and a person or department that is responsible for getting the tactics fulfilled. A finished plan is a beautiful thing. While having a professional moderator is helpful, you can do it yourself if a trained go-between isn't available.

Last, which is as important as everything that went before it, is a regular review of the plan, at least monthly. Using Microsoft Office Project to track tactic completion helps ensure that the plan will be completed. Hold everyone accountable for completing the plan. Celebrate when each objective has been reached because the strategies and tactics have been completed on time and on budget.

With a solid marketing plan, you won't end up someplace else; you know exactly where you're going.

Section Seven

Internet
Marketing

The march of technology started off as a good idea. Use this thing some techno geeks invented called the Internet to promote your business. Advertise your products and services, just like the yellow pages, but do it online. Attract the modern consumer and make gobs and gobs of money. Sound familiar?

Somewhere along the way the march turned crazy. What used to be a simple idea became extremely complex. Instead of getting a simple web site built in a day or so, you were advised to first conduct a three-day internet strategy session. In order to compete against your competitor's web site, you now needed graphic artists, web site designers, and internet marketing specialists. You were asked to explain your page view growth strategy, how many eyeballs you were attracting, how many "click-throughs" were being logged, and your online conversion rate. You had to wonder, what does this have to do with my bottom line?

In one word, Plenty!

Forrester Research says sales over the internet have increased every year by at least 20% and are currently estimated for year 2008 at $310 billion dollars. And here's a startling fact: only 33% of the world population is currently using the internet! Talk about a high-growth opportunity! If only we could understand how to use it...

The following section will give you some great ideas about how to use the Internet to drive profits to your business and attract thousands of new buyers.

Chapter **39**

Introduction to Internet Marketing

By Judy Key Johnson

Imagine a billion people, which is about the number of Internet users in the world in 2007. You are looking for customers for your company, which offers surfing lessons in California and Costa Rica, from among this billion. How do you find them, or – perhaps a better question – how do they find you?

OPTION 1 – Traditional marketing, which involves advertising in publications and distributing flyers for your service, hoping to find people who want to attend surf camp. It's not only expensive; it's like finding a needle in a haystack.

OPTION 2 – Internet marketing, in which people wanting to find a surf camp type "surf school" or "surf lessons" into Google and find www.surfschool.net on page 1 of their search results. They click on the link, like what they see on the web site and register online or call the company.

1,500% Sales Increase in Three Years

Rick Walker, president of Corky Carroll's Surf School, started using Internet Marketing in 2002. "Before using search engine optimization (SEO) we were selling about 12 of our high-margin, one-week learn-to-surf in Costa Rica packages per year. In the first year of implementing SEO, our Costa Rica business quadrupled, the second year it doubled again, and the third year it even doubled from that for a three-year increase of over 1,500%." The cost of Rick's SEO service? About $500 a month.

Internet Advertising – Lower Cost per Sales Lead

Corky Carroll's Surf School is one of the companies fueling the meteoric rise in Internet Marketing, which grabbed $15 billion in U.S. advertising dollars in 2006, exceeding 5% of total media placement revenue for the first time and an increase of 33% over 2005 (Interactive Advertising Bureau).

Internet advertising is growing so quickly because it's much more cost effective than traditional advertising in most circumstances. Piper Jaffray &

Co., a leading market analyst firm, estimates that the cost per lead for traditional marketing channels is $9.94 for direct mail and $1.18 for Yellow Pages ®, while for Internet advertising it is $2.00 for banner ads, $0.55 for email marketing and $0.45 for search engine marketing.

The advertising spend is driven by the growth in Internet usage, up 10% from December 2005 to December 2006 (comScore Networks), with search being the largest area of gain, followed by multimedia (video and music), community (MySpace, Facebook), email, and games.

It's important for small companies not to be intimidated by these large numbers because the key components of Internet Marketing apply to both small businesses, such as Corky Carroll's Surf School, and to giants of the Internet like Best Buy and Land's End. This article presents an introduction to Internet Marketing that you can apply to your business.

Internet Marketing as a marketing discipline is less than 15 years old and uses much more sophisticated technology than traditional marketing. However, the programs rely on the same three basic marketing activities:

1. Get 'em
2. Keep 'em
3. Sell 'em

Get 'Em - Help Prospects Find Your Web Site

Over 73% of all web sites are found through search engines (Forrester Research). The number of searches is staggering; there were more than six billion searches in the U.S. in the single month of December 2006. Google accounted for 67% of all queries worldwide in April 2007 (Nielsen/NetRatings.com), up 20 points in the past two years, while Yahoo has tumbled to 19% and *msn* to 8%.

There are many options in Internet advertising – banner advertising, search engine marketing, email marketing lists and specialty programs like viral marketing campaigns, blogging, and social networking promotions. Banner advertising, the first option to be adopted, moved the concept of print advertising over to the new medium of the Internet. In recent years, search engine marketing has gained the top position in advertising spend because it is a good place for businesses to start their lead generation campaigns.

Keep 'Em – Can Your Web Site Hold Their Interest?

Once a lead comes to your site, via search engine marketing or other lead generation techniques, it's up to the web site to keep them long enough to trigger an action that establishes a relationship with your company.

The bar keeps rising for web sites. Four years ago simply having a web site was good enough to trigger an action. Now web sites need to have much more compelling content, easy navigation and use of multiple media such as flash movies and embedded videos.

Sell 'Em – The Conversion

Too often companies don't spend enough time deciding what action they want people to take when they get to the web site nor do they think about how to make that action as compelling as possible.

Do you know how many people view your web site in a month and what percentage of them are "converted" (take the action that you desire, such as filling out a form for additional information or ordering a product)?

We will discuss mining the information in your web site log in a later chapter. As a rule of thumb, conversion rates from search engine marketing are in the range of 2% to 4%, but targets vary widely depending on the conversion activity. Downloading a free video game would have a much higher rate than, say, signing up for a one-week surfing trip to Costa Rica.

An Integrated Internet Marketing Plan

The key to increasing sales through Internet Marketing is to have an end-to-end plan for getting, keeping, and selling prospects, weighing the many different tools and programs that are available.

Internet Marketing can provide more leads and sales at a lower cost than traditional marketing because of the targeted, opt-in nature of the Internet. There is a window of opportunity to seize business using these new techniques and strategies.

Chapter 40

PPC or SEO? Two Very Different Lead Generation Tools

By Judy Key Johnson

Carl Kunkleman, Vice President of Sales for the safety consulting firm KPA, thinks search engine optimization (SEO) is the best lead generation program he's ever used. It's easy to understand his enthusiasm. Leads coming in through the company web site due to SEO have a 5X greater close rate and take 1/10 the time to close compared to leads from his traditional sources such as cold calling prospect lists. He pays his SEO vendor under $1,000 a month.

On the other hand, when I was Vice President of Marketing for a baseball video game company, we implemented an extensive pay per click (PPC) campaign during the beta phase of our product in order to test different advertising messages against different player demographics. This campaign cost us about $40,000 for six months.

Which is better, SEO or PPC? One is not inherently better than the other, but there is almost always a better choice for your situation. Both forms of search engine marketing use search engines to bring people to your web site link, but otherwise they are very different.

If you think of Google as a newspaper, then PPC is an ad, paid for by an advertiser, and SEO is a news article, which is published solely at the discretion of the newspaper but which can be influenced by a persuasive PR firm.

PPC – the more you pay the more visibility you get

With Pay Per Click a company purchases ad space, as it wants, through Google Ad Words, Yahoo, or on smaller search engines, sometimes with very targeted viewers. Advertisers select specific keyword phrases, decide how much they want to bid for each keyword phrase on each search engine, and pay the search engine each time someone clicks on that word in the "Sponsored Link" section of Google and other search engines. Price per word varies with the popularity of the word and the position of the word on the search engine page. The top ad on page 1 of Google will cost a lot more than getting the #4 position. These prices are very fluid, changing with real-time bidding.

Unlike a newspaper ad, where you pay a fixed fee regardless of how many people view the ad, pay per click is just that – pay per click. Each time someone clicks on the web site a charge, typically ranging from 10 cents to 10 dollars, is paid to the search engine. The more clicks on an advertiser's web site link, the more the advertiser pays.

Of course, your competitor might think it's a good idea for you to be spending your PPC money on clicks that THEY originate and what's to stop them from clicking on your Sponsored Links as often as they want? There's a term for this: "click fraud." Competitors, or even web sites that are paid to host PPC ads, might click on your links themselves and drive up your costs. Click fraud rates are estimated to be as high as 30%, a number strongly disputed by Google, which pegs the number at around 0.2%.

SEO – fighting your way toward to the top of Google

There are some things that money can't buy, and a top ranking on Google is one of them. Google has a complex algorithm of about 160 variables that determine whether a company's web site appears as the #1 or #1,000,000 listing. They don't publish their determinants, which include obvious factors such as frequency of use of the keyword phrases, longevity of the web site, size of the web site, popularity of the web site, and some obscure technical criteria, and they are believed to modify 5-15% of the determinants each month. SEO is also called "natural" or "organic" search, because the position itself cannot be purchased.

SEO is the science, and art, of getting a web site ranked high in Google and other search engines by a combination of programming and content techniques. SEO firms tend to charge a fixed fee regardless of the number of hits on your web site, which makes budgeting more predictable. Fees start as low as $500 a month and require no changes to the web site, making SEO typically the best value of all Internet advertising options.

Here are some factors to consider in selecting when to use PPC and when to use SEO:

Web sites listed in the regular pages of search engine results have a conversion rate about four times higher than in the sponsored (PPC) section, for the same reason that people view paid ads with more skepticism than personal referral.

1. **How quickly do you want results?** Speed is the biggest advantage of PPC. The moment you start paying the search engine for the keyword phrase and ranking position you want, it's yours. It generally takes three to six months to get an SEO ranking on page 1 of Google, if you can get it at all. With SEO advance planning is a

must so if you want to launch a new product in six months you must act now.

2. **How important is cost per lead?** SEO leads are much less expensive than PPC in most cases. Just as newspaper readers tend to skip the ads and read the articles, fewer people look at the "sponsored links" on the top row or right column of a search engine page as opposed to the SEO section that dominates the page. Seventy-three percent of Google users select an SEO link over a PPC link when they do a search. Also, whereas in PPC the advertiser literally pays for each click, SEO is priced at a fixed rate for the service, so you are not paying more per lead. The bottom line is that, assuming you are not a very small advertiser who manages your PPC campaign yourself, SEO is three to seven times less expensive per lead than PPC.

3. **Are you flexible in the keyword phrases?** Every keyword phrase is for sale in PPC. If you care to spend the money, you can have the #1 Sponsored Link position in Google for any phrase you like. With SEO the emphasis is on selecting less obvious phrases used by your target audience, generally terms that are searched less frequently than the initial obvious phrases but with a high likelihood of scoring a page 1 or 2 Google ranking. SEO firms use tools to find these phrases and to model the likely results.

4. **How much time do you want to spend?** SEO will require almost none of your time once you select the initial phrases and make content modifications to your web site, if you choose to take that extra step to improve your rankings. You pay an SEO vendor and they do all the work of getting and keeping your rankings high. You can manage your own PPC campaign with Google Adwords or other programs, but there's a learning curve and you need to manage it on a daily basis because your credit card is being charged automatically. Most companies that are not very small hire PPC administrators who tend to be expensive because the work is very specialized, time-consuming and needs constant monitoring.

Bottom line

SEO provides the biggest "bang for the buck" in generating traffic from search engines, but there is no way around the three to six month startup time for page 1 or 2 Google rankings and you need to be flexible in the keyword phrases that you select. If you need immediate results, for market research or for a short term lead generation campaign, go for PPC.

Chapter 41

How to Improve
Your Search Engine Rankings

By Judy Key Johnson

When looking for a product or service on Google, how often do you look beyond the first or second page? Data shows that only 37% of all searches extend to page 2, and only 7% to page 3. While the #1 position in Google gives tremendous bragging rights, the fact is that 83% of all people look at the first five entries in Google.

But enough about the statistics of page rankings. You already know that you want your web site to be ranked as high as possible. With the tremendous economic value of high search engine rankings, more and more companies are hiring search engine optimization firms. There are so many tricks of the trade, often involving behind-the-scenes programming, that no the business professional, or even a company's webmaster, can beat search engine professionals in the rankings game.

Google has about 160 criteria that go into determining the ranking for each search term for each web site on the World Wide Web. These criteria are not announced and are constantly changing. It is believed that 10% to 15% of the criteria change monthly. Search engine optimization companies work with a wide variety of these criteria, many of which involve behind-the-scenes software techniques beyond the capability of the general business owner or webmaster. There are, however, a number of content-related actions that you can take to improve your search engine rankings regardless of whether you also have professional optimization or not.

Your first step is to determine the keyword phrases that your target audience is likely to use to find your web site. A brainstorming session with your sales and marketing team is often a good way to start creating the list; free tools on the Internet, such as Wordtracker (www.wordtracker.com), can help you refine the phrases. Once you determine your target phrases and benchmark the current ranking for each term, you're ready to start improving your rankings.

Web site techniques that improve search engine rankings:

1. **Focus on the Home page.** Search engines weigh the Home page much higher than the other pages in determining the rankings for keyword phrases. The design of the home page should support enough text to include key phrases. Google determines the write-up on the company descriptor that appears on the search engine page. They pull that text primarily from your home page.

2. **Frequent use of keyword phrases.** Search engines have a specific goal, which is to deliver the best possible content experience relevant to the keyword phrase that a user types in. They are looking, through automated techniques, at the number of times the keyword appears on a web site, with an emphasis on the top-level navigation pages. The weighting for frequency of use of a search term (known as "keyword density" in SEO jargon) may tempt one to use a technique known as "cloaking," in which a keyword phrases is repeated, as often as 100 times, on a Web page in the same color as the background so that it is not visible to the reader but is read by the search engines. Don't do this. Cloaking is considered an illegal technique by the search engines. If you are caught, your site may be de-listed, which means no ranking at all. It's far better to follow these tips, which are all legal.

3. **Use of keywords in page headings**. The search engines reason that if a keyword phrase is used in a heading, the page content is focused on that topic. They therefore give the site extra "points" in determining the ranking for a term if that term appears in a heading.

4. **Use of keywords in first and last paragraph**. The position of a keyword on the Web page influences the ranking index. For the best rankings, the term should appear in the first and last paragraphs. If you think like Google you will see the logic that if a term appears in the first and last paragraph, the content on that page is probably focused on that term.

5. **Create web pages for specific search terms**. Every company has multiple keyword phrases it wants ranked high. You can't squeeze them all onto the Home page with a heavy emphasis on each phrase. Instead create a site map in which your keyword phrases have their own pages, and then follow the above rules. If you are doing paid search (also known as Pay Per Click, such as Google Adwords) you will have created landing pages. You can use those landing pages for this purpose.

6. **Expand the number of links into your web site**. Search engines increase rankings for web sites with lots of inward links—that is, other web sites that link into your site. However, and this is critical, links vary widely in their impact in the search engine ranking

algorithms. Links from large, credible web sites, such as IBM, ESPN, or Harvard University, will help your rankings much more than from small sites. At the extreme, an illegal ranking improvement technique known as "link farming," in which you pay a fee for many links to be joined to your site, can get you de-listed. Make sure that businesses and associations with whom you have a legitimate business interest, such as distributors of your products and professional associations, include a link to your web site. It can help your rankings and, more importantly, lead more people to your site.

Web site techniques that damage your search engine ranking:
1. **All-Flash Home page**. Search engines don't read Adobe® Flash® animation, and they give greater weight to the content of the Home page. Therefore an all-Flash home page is a double whammy. You can certainly have Flash on your Home page—in fact, I recommend it for visual interest. However, be sure to leave room for text and use that text space for rich content.
2. **"Artsy" text and stories on the Home page**. To repeat myself, you need to balance sales effectiveness against tuning to get high rankings. After writing the content that you think is most effective, step back and check that it also includes the keyword phrases that you want well ranked.

Follow these few simple rules and you will increase your search engine ranking and deliver a clear and focused message about your services.

Chapter **42**

What's Hot, and What's Not, in Web Sites

By Judy Key Johnson

Forget the rule of thumb that you have 15 seconds to make a positive impression with your web site or the viewer will move on. As people increasingly use search engines to locate vendors, they make even quicker decisions as they move down Google rankings, starting with #1.

If your web site looks out of date—the digital equivalent of a polyester leisure suit—the Web surfer may make a snap judgment that your business is equally out of date and unsuccessful and move on to a competitor's site.

Here are some of the latest trends in web sites.

Trend #1. Full-motion Video.

The cost of video production has dropped to the point of affordability for most companies, with prices for a professionally filmed and edited 15- to 30-second clip ranging from $3,000 to $10,000, including professional actors and a soundtrack. Video clips are a wonderful way to communicate exactly the message that you want to get across and have a much higher emotional impact than text and stock photography.

Video is especially effective for providers of personal services, such as medical specialists or consultants, where the business needs to establish a personal connection with the viewer. When a web site receives many viewers through search engines and there is no prior relationship between the searcher and the company, a video is a great way to help viewers get to know you quickly.

A bunion surgeon who routinely invested heavily in pay-per-click advertising found that sales leads from his web site more than doubled after he added a welcome video to his home page. This physician subsequently enhanced his site with a series of videos illustrating his services and his satisfied patients and grew his business by millions of dollars a year.

Trend #2. Secondary Navigation.

The earliest web sites established a single, common navigation scheme that remains in use today and is very comfortable for Web views. It's generally a variation of *Home, About Us, Services, Press, Clients/Industries, Contact Us*. There is a lot to be said for using the expected navigation; the viewer can quickly go to the area of interest.

However, as marketing gets more and more targeted, refining specific messages and services to micro-demographics, the use of secondary navigation is increasingly common. This navigation may, for a B2B site, list the different buyer roles (engineer, CFO, teachers) or industries (legal, entertainment, aviation), product lines (hoses, harnesses, clamps) or many other categories. Often these categories and sub categories are displayed as vertical navigation or as a second horizontal navigation scheme.

As you plan your web site navigation, remember that each click is your enemy, with viewership falling dramatically with each required click before the viewer finds the information that will compel him to take a conversion action, such as requesting additional information. Secondary navigation is an excellent way to increase the stickiness of your web site.

Trend #3. Flash Animation.

If you invest in a new web site these days and you don't include Flash® animation, your site will look out of date before it even goes live.

Forget about the common objections to Flash—"takes too much bandwidth," "my viewers don't have a flash player installed," "makes the site too slow to load." None of these are true anymore; even old PCs and dial-up bandwidths can support modern Flash animation and brief Flash movies. The cost of developing a simple flash animation is just a few hundred dollars.

Trend #4. Custom Photography.

OK, this is a pet project of mine. I admit it. Now that web sites like www.istockphoto.com have put the price of high-quality stock photography into the $10 price range, images of the smiling man in a suit shaking hands with another smiling person of a dissimilar gender, ethnicity and/or age range seem to be on every other home page in the B2B space. You can spot stock photography a mile away; it is well lit, well posed, and looks the same on your web site as on all your competitors' sites.

Come on! You can hire a professional photographer for $500 to $1,000 and end up with a portfolio of custom photographs that you can use for your web site and other marketing collateral. Determine your site map and plan the photos carefully in advance of the photo shoot for maximum benefit. I guarantee your site will reflect your company's individuality and create a more personal relationship at first glance.

Trend #5. More Concise Text.

The first web sites were little more than online brochures with lots of text extending well below the screen viewable without scrolling. Over time, Internet marketers learned the type of text that is most effective for web sites and that writing for web sites is far different than writing for brochures.

Trend #6. Search Engine Friendly.

In a previous chapter we discussed web site techniques you can use to increase your search engine rankings and other techniques to avoid.

Web site viewing patterns have also changed. Search engine usage has skyrocketed, viewer attention spans are much shorter and there are many more portable PCs with small screen sizes than a decade ago when corporate web sites became common.

The Home page, in particular, has to grab the attention of Web searchers in 10 seconds, and should have a small amount of clear, compelling text, coupled with one or more effective visual images.

The bottom line: consider the economic value of your web site and invest accordingly. A hyper-effective web site can bring in tens or hundreds of thousands of dollars in additional income or even a million dollars more for a certain bunion surgeon in Southern California.

Chapter 43

Hidden Treasure in Your Web Log

By Judy Key Johnson

The online videogame producer had a life-or-death problem. No major product enhancements were planned for the next year and the company's sole source of revenue was tied to the number of visitors to the web site and the game. Fundraising was a necessity but how to generate enthusiasm for a game that so few people played?

With limited marketing dollars, the company needed to make some smart, low-cost choices about how to promote the game, which was enthusiastically, even obsessively, played by the few thousand people who had discovered it.

With guidance from an Internet marketing expert, the producer stopped operating solely on instinct and instead made business decisions based on careful daily interpretation of web site usage data. The company then deployed the targeted marketing actions, watched the results and fine tuned the programs frequently based on data received.

The result was that monthly page views skyrocketed from 75,000 to 950,000 in less than a year, advertising revenue increased accordingly and the company successfully raised additional investment funds.

The cost for the Web log data that was the basis for this turnaround — free Web logs and an additional Web statistic program—was less than $300 a month. These same tools are available to you.

Web Log Data—Free and Yours for the Asking

Every web site is hosted either on your company's own server or on a hosting service such as EarthLink or GoDaddy. As part of the service a log is run 24/7, recording a wide array of data about the activity in, out, and inside your site by visitors.

This data can be yours for the asking, without charge, either as a periodic report or with access so that you can view the reports yourself at any time. Many hosting companies or webmasters don't mention the availability of this information. They may never talk with the business personnel. However, this data is a goldmine of business information.

You can also download the Google Web Analytics toolbar, which is free and easy to use.

What's in a web log?

The information in a basic Web log is searchable by time period with a month as the default and includes:

- Number of page views
- Number of unique viewers
- Page views by time of day
- Page views by day of the week
- Number of views of each web site page
- Number of hits for each search engine
- Number of searches for different keyword phrases
- Number and types of visitors' browsers and operating systems

Additional Web Data, Still A Great Value

More comprehensive web site tools are available, often for a monthly fee ranging from $100 to $500. Many companies charge by the number of page views on the site. One of the most established of such vendors is WebTrends, although there are many other firms offering products at lower prices. A shareware product called Phlogger is a low-cost alternative. Information provided by these supplemental tools can include:

- Email addresses of visitors to the site
- Length of time each page is visited
- The URL path flow of visitors (this is very valuable in streamlining the steps to the conversion action)
- Change (decrease) in click-throughs along a URL path flow

Converting Data Into Action

The video game company formed a SWAT team of an Internet marketing consultant, the videogame player community advocate, the webmaster and the product manager. The team met daily to study the Web logs and turn their findings into immediate action.

Among the changes were to streamline the game registration process, which was designed by a "theorist" who wanted to collect lots of information before allowing game play. The Web logs proved that less than 10% of the people who initially started the signup process completed the action due to the cumbersome design. The Web analytics highlighted the steps that had the highest dropout rate, allowing the product manager to focus on the high-impact areas and implement and re-test the results. Ultimately, after a rapid iterative set of designs, the retention rate was above 50%, which was critical to growing the core membership of game players.

The Web logs also showed the countries outside of the North America where the game was most popular. The company, which previously only hosted special events and provided customer support during US hours, started thinking globally. Customer support hours were significantly expanded, online competitions were held for each geographic area and cross-geography competitions became a huge hit. The results were not only growth in the number of players but a company that was much more attractive to investors and to international advertisers.

Internet Marketing – Combo Pack

While the elements of traditional marketing — messaging, customer feedback, and return on investment — apply to Internet marketing, the programs and tools are definitely from the 21st century. Search engine marketing — search engine optimization and pay-per-click — have gotten very sophisticated in the past five years. Early Internet marketing programs, such as banner advertising, have been replaced by much more sophisticated customer-facing techniques tuned to targeted demographics. Web analytic tools provide much of the data to make informed, fast-paced decisions.

Companies that master Internet marketing quickly, such as the online videogame company, will leave their slower-moving competitors far behind.

Chapter **44**

Web 2.0: Expanding Internet Marketing

By Judy Key Johnson

You have probably accepted the fact that your company web site will always be a work in progress. The notion that you create a web site once has been replaced by the reality that your web site needs frequent attention to both content and design.

This chapter is devoted to educating you about Web 2.0 and helping you evaluate its applicability to your business needs.

Web 2.0 is a broad term describing a major shift in the approach and style of web site design. Despite the rather techie-sounding name, Web 2.0 is not a technology but rather an approach to a web site as a social community that facilitates collaboration and sharing of information among visitors to the site. The content of a Web 2.0 style web site is no longer controlled solely by the company. Instead the user community interacts with and indeed places content on the site.

A set of web site tools, such as blogs, social media, RSS feeds, video blogs, wikis and interactive games, are used to implement a Web 2.0 strategy. Three of the most fundamental techniques that apply to corporate web sites are blogs, social media, and RSS feeds.

Blogs – The user speaks up on your web site.

A blog (abbreviation of web log) is a web site or section of a web site which displays one or more participant entries. These entries are generally shown with the current entry at the top of the column. Entries are posted with great frequency, typically a minimum of every few days. The most popular blogs may attract hundreds of blog postings in a day.

In a consumer blog, such as blogs about a particular video game or an athletic team, the writing style is casual and typically uncensored, the author is generally identified by a pseudonym and writers spend a great deal of time commenting upon one another's web posts.

Corporate blogs are different in that a company employee maintains the blog and generally posts comments on a regular basis. Because the nature of a blog is user participation (otherwise it would simply be a company column on the web site), entries may be made by outside participants. The company has, because of its web site administration capabilities, the ability to edit or remove blog entries. Editing blogs, however, is counter to the free-exchange premise of blogs and users will quickly detect such editing.

To blog or not to blog?

Does your company truly want to open itself up to a two-way dialog in an open forum? With a blog, as with other elements of Web 2.0, a company is making the decision to loosen control of the company brand and turn it into more of a dialog, with consumers participating in defining the brand.

It is vital that the CEO and board agree on the ground rules for your company blog because a company blog will raise policy questions that have probably never been addressed.

Here are some questions that need to be answered:

1. What is the business advantage that you wish to achieve by creating a blog? Establishing the domain expertise of your company as evidenced by the knowledgeable commentary that you post on a frequent basis? Credibility for your company as a web-savvy organization open to free-flowing discussion? Content that brings more people to your web site more frequently? Unfiltered, direct feedback to your company?

2. If you build it, will they come? Some topics are inherently much more suited to blogs than others. Consumer products are a natural. People are passionate about the products they use in their personal lives. A small group of fanatics will blog about almost anything you can buy in a store. B2B products need to be weighted more carefully. Simply put, do people care enough about your products, services or topics aligned with those products, for a blog to be successful, which means attract frequent entries? Industrial fasteners may attract bloggers, but then maybe not. If not, that's OK. It just means that a blog isn't a marketing vehicle that is suitable to your company.

3. Are you willing to commit permanent resources to generate copy, ideally on a daily basis, for your blog? Even if you don't post every day, your blog needs to be scrutinized every day by a company representative. A blog can quickly veer off in a negative direction, with a thread of comments appearing within just a few hours. You will want to monitor the site evenings and weekends because your blog is open for business 24/7.

4. What is your policy on editing or removing negative or misleading comments on your blog? How will you announce that policy to the user community? How frequently will you monitor the site

(including off-work hours)? Once a comment is posted it may spread virally outside of the blog. Most companies in the pre-blog era had near total control of the information made available on the company and its products. Everything changes with Web 2.0 and nowhere more than with a blog on your web site.

5. Another aspect of a blogging strategy is the monitoring and possible contribution to blogs where your company wishes to be favorably mentioned. These may be user experience sites that review products or even "flame" sites staffed by irate users. There are many decisions to make, from anonymously posting comments favorable to your products (unethical) to employing a "pay per blog" company that hires outsiders to write about your product on third party sites (also unethical, unless disclosed). Even if you don't set up a blog on your company web site, you will want to identify and monitor blogs that mention your products (home appliances and home computer products incur huge wrath when they fail to perform as promised).

If you decide to start a blog, do your research on best practices for blogs. You need to create a blog strategy. You're in new territory now.

Social Media

YouTube, MySpace, Facebook, Digg, and Flickr are all examples of social media. These web sites allow the exchange of text, graphic, and sound content between users, generally within community groups that define themselves and change over time.

Over a billion people worldwide have established an identity on one or more social networks. Web-savvy marketing plans can achieve an almost unimaginable visibility boost if you catch the attention of a social network. Movies, consumer products, and even political campaigns hire experts to craft sophisticated strategies to present their messages in social networks.

Questions to ask yourself before integrating social media into your corporate brand management strategy:

1. Does my target audience use social networks? Let's face it, MySpace and YouTube are primarily used by the under 30 crowd and the goods and services that catch the attention of those users are primarily consumer products, such as movies and music. If your company specializes in selling aircraft hoses to commercial airlines, social networks are unlikely to be a relevant part of your marketing plan.
2. As with blogs, the cost/benefit analysis of participating in a social network needs to be evaluated. Are you willing to dedicate resources to contribute to and monitor the content?

RSS Feeds

A RSS feed (RSS stand for "Real Simple Syndication" or Rich Site Summary) is a data format that provides web site visitors with frequently updated content that people subscribe to. One generally sees a small rectangle RSS somewhere on the Home page of a web site. You can think of a RSS feed as a near-continuous flow of information. Content of an RSS feed, also called a web feed, generally is a combination of other content services (web aggregators) and original content.

Web users like RSS feeds because, unlike email newsletters, they can subscribe to them without providing their email address. This reduces problems with spam, viruses, phishing and identity theft. Also, RSS subscribers can unsubscribe to many content sources provided in a single web feed with a single unsubscribe action that they can control.

There are many advantages to establishing your web site as the "go to" place for current information related to a topic:

1. You establish your company as a domain expert, which adds credibility, boosting the perceived value of your goods and services.
2. You keep your company top-of-mind with customers and prospects, who return to your web site on a regular basis to see what's new in the industry on the RSS feed.
3. By boosting web site hits, you increase your ranking on the search engines.
4. If web site advertising is part of your revenue, then more web visitors translates directly into more revenue.

Unfortunately, the strategy "let's establish our web site as the place to go for industry information" isn't exactly an original concept and the barrier to entry is very low. Sometimes it seems that every other startup has as its strategy, "to be the leading site for information about ****."

Unlike blogs and social networks, RSS feeds don't have the uncertainty of user generated-content. RSS feeds are one-way from the RSS provider to the subscribers. However, as with all Web 2.0 techniques, RSS feeds require constant attention; that is the expectation of user-interaction tools.

Web 2.0 – Your Next Step

User interaction over the internet is the heart of Web 2.0. The tools and techniques will continue to expand. After all, over a billion people are online and each is empowered to interact on Web 2.0-enabled web sites.

The question for most companies is not if you will adopt Web 2.0, but when and which techniques will you employ first. Web 2.0 brings a significant change to the concept of marketing with both a loss of control and an opportunity to be closer to your users than ever before in a candid dialog. It is a revolution that cannot be ignored.

Section Eight

Business Development

According to industry statistics, 80% of new businesses fail in their first five years of business? Care to guess why?

It's a failure to acquire new customers, which leads to lack of INCOME.

That should come as no big surprise. However, here's another fact. When it comes to established businesses, 78% of business failures can be attributed to two things: Poor leadership or lack of planning, both of which directly relate to enormous problems attracting new business.

The lifeblood of any business is new customers! Attracting them and interesting them in your products or services has never been more critical to your success. Today's ultra-competitive environment makes it ever more difficult. It's getting harder and harder to show WHY prospects should choose to do business with your company rather than with the hundreds of other companies with very similar products and messages.

The old days of simply handing the phone book to eager salesmen and telling them to get out there and "pound the pavement" are long gone. Cold calling today produces such dismal results that most sales teams have banned the practice. It's no longer "just a numbers game." Access to decision makers has become the main challenge. Corporate leaders are increasingly adopting sophisticated defenses against being contacted. The gatekeepers today are fiercely trained and often electronic.

Given this challenging environment, how should you put together a successful business development plan? What works today and what doesn't? What's the secret to generating volumes of qualified leads?

The following section contains dozens of ideas to help you win new business. Somewhere out there dozens of new customers eagerly await your call. Let us help you find them!

Chapter **45**

Building Valuable Connections Inside and Out

By Patrick McClure

No one achieves excellence on their own. Whether your business is developing a meaningful career, creating a loving family, coming up with an innovative idea, crafting a work of art, or developing a vast commercial empire, your success depends on others and theirs depends on you.

Walt Disney said, "You can dream, create, design, and build the most wonderful idea in the world, but it requires people to make the dream a reality."

The father of Mickey Mouse, Disneyland and the Epcot center knew what he was talking about. He was a creative genius with innovative ideas, tremendous energy, and the will to succeed. Yet without others joining his cause, his best ideas would have died before ever becoming reality.

You may be experiencing the same thing. You have good ideas, great experience, valuable insights, and tremendous energy. You've taken the initiative and launched your own business. Now, with full confidence and optimism, you expect the world to beat a path to your door. And so you wait. And wait. And wait some more.

What you need to do is build a team! You need to establish a network of valuable connections who work together to help each other. You need to create an army of advocates that willingly take the initiative to recommend your company to whomever they meet. Likewise they need YOU on their team to recommend their services.

Every person on the team can win the game if they all work together for the common good. Every person can achieve their goals by helping each other.

The key to success in life and in business is to build valuable connections!

There are two deceptively simple steps to do this:

1. Build Connections

2. Create Value

It's all about Building Connections and Creating Value.

To accelerate performance you must first make a connection.

On a personal level, we spend 90% of our lives alone, living in fear and loneliness. We simply assume that everyone else is "normal and that we're the only ones who have these strange feelings of alienation." We know, deep down inside, that we don't belong here and that we never will. Everyone else seems to be happier, more adjusted, more affluent and more satisfied with the way things are going.

Perhaps Robert Heinlein was correct when he wrote his science-fiction classic *Stranger in a Strange Land*. His main character, Michael Valentine Smith, was raised by Martians and had somehow developed highly-evolved skills including mental telepathy. When meeting people from this planet for the first time, he noticed how lonely and unhappy they appeared to be. There was no bond, no connection between them. They were all strangers, even to each other.

These concepts are equally relevant to the business world. Getting connected and staying connected has never been more important. Companies spend millions of dollars annually in an attempt to make a connection with their consumers. Besides media and advertising exposure, use a plethora of technologically-enabled solutions such as web sites, blogs, podcasts, and newsletters.

Consumers and businesses have adopted defensive strategies to filter out unwanted connections (spam) and to spot the desired communications with sophisticated electronic defense systems such as firewalls, denied lists, voicemail, and elaborate security systems to protect their resources and people.

The driving goal of most business communication is to create visibility (i.e. connection with) your potential consumers. Success in business demands that you get over internal loneliness and self-centeredness and focus your energy and messages outside, on your customers.

Your success in business, in your career and in your life is dependant upon your ability to create value AND establish new connections. Building your personal team requires a deep understanding and mastery of the process of building valuable connections.

Chapter 46

Click: You Just Lost your Audience

By Patrick McClure

We live today in the Instant Messaging generation and I'm afraid the majority of you aren't getting the message! Today's communication traffic travels at supersonic speed and many of us aren't moving that fast! If we can't receive the message, how on earth can we expect to deliver our message?

Whether you are speaking, presenting, or writing, your audience will make decisions FAST about whether they should give you their attention. They are constantly wondering WIFM (What's in it for me?) If you don't give them a good answer to that question, they will "click" you off!

Where's the remote?

Practically everyone in America owns a remote control. I'm sure each of you has about six to ten of them lying around your living room. It gives you instant access to and control over every one of the channels on your multimedia entertainment system. With this device, you can click through about 800 channels in less than two minutes. Click, access for about five seconds, and move on.

The average Internet user takes six seconds to scan a new page and decide whether they should click through to another choice from that page or just move on to another site.

I receive about 100 emails on an average day. I also receive about 10 newsletters. For my peace of mind, I must make near-instant decisions on what to read and why.

On my cell phone/personal data assistant, I can scan an instant message or an email and decide within seconds whether to download or delete. In seconds. With one hand, many of today's adept children (not me) can reply in text messaging shorthand (net lingo), again in seconds. And sometimes while driving the car or in the classroom.

People today decide within seconds what they will listen to, watch, read, or experience. Within seconds! Never before in history has it been possible for so much information to arrive so fast and in such quantity. People are frankly overwhelmed with information!

Research conducted by some of the top speakers in the world, members of the National Speaker's Association, has confirmed that you have only about 30 seconds to grab the audience's attention and convince them you are worthy of their attention before they click to something else. In those first 30 seconds, your audience will hopefully decide three critical facts:

- This speaker is different.
- I think they might have something valuable to listen to.
- I'm not leaving.

Let's assume you have been given the chance to present. You have an audience. They will stay in their chairs and give you their attention if they hear a compelling message from you, something that grabs their attention, and something that leads them to believe you are worth listening to. You have 30 seconds to answer the BIG question in their mind: What's in it for me?

Yet what does the typical speaker do in the first two minutes of their speech? Here's a short list. See if you recognize yourself:

- Thank the person who introduced you.
- Thank the group for inviting you.
- Apologize for how unprepared you are.
- Apologize for not being very good at this.
- Tell them you didn't have much time to prepare.
- Make some other excuses.
- Tell a long-winded story about your airline/taxi/train to the meeting.
- Read a joke you just copied over the internet.
- Shuffle through your notes, quickly reviewing them.
- Sip a glass of water.
- Adjust your glasses.
- Adjust your tie.
- Look at your watch.
- Clear your throat.
- ALL OF THE ABOVE

How many of the above do you do?

Get to the point.

Today's instant messaging generation doesn't have the patience to wait. Get to the point QUICKLY and convince your audience that you will not waste their time. Grab their attention right off the bat with something that is attention getting, startling, provocative and interesting to THEM. In job interviews, casual conversation and meetings with smaller groups, you still need to GET to the point fast. People have limited attention spans and time is precious.

By the way, never assume that having an audience sitting patiently in their chairs is proof that you have earned their undivided attention. Most people learned long ago to sit still, focus their eyes on a teacher/speaker and zone out to their favorite fantasy world. The key question is this: are they actively engaged and participating in the presentation?

These points apply equally to the written word. The typical consumer is hammered with a barrage of media from multiple sources. What is it that will convince the reader to read your message rather than the thousands of others? What's so important, so interesting, so compelling about your message? I have stacks of books and magazines on my "reading pile." What will convince me to read YOUR book first, rather than all the others?

Remember to analyze your audience and understand what makes them tick. What is important to them and why? Do your research! When you write or speak, remember to appeal to the commonly held values of that group. If you are speaking or writing to a group of veterans, appeal to their commonly held values of patriotism, duty to county, and service. If you're speaking or writing to high school students, talk about school spirit, the latest song or dance, and their upcoming football game.

Then determine your objective and organize your speech or article to deliver the key important points relative to your objective. Organize it around your common theme.

Remember :

- State it in the first 30 seconds of your speech.
- Write it in the first few paragraphs of your article.
- List it on the title page of your web site.
- Key it into the first line of your text message.
- Print it in the subject line of your email.
- Speak it in the first few seconds of your voicemail.

Move FAST to capture their attention. Don't become just another Click.

Chapter 47

Wasting Time on the Wrong People

By Patrick McClure

"It's a good idea not to major in minor things."   *--Anthony Robbins*

Stop wasting your time on the wrong people.

Billions of people and millions of companies exist on this planet. Among them is the perfect, ideal customer waiting to hear from you. Ahead of you is the world's easiest sale, a certified "bluebird."

Find that person and sell to them!

Don't waste valuable time selling to a company that doesn't need your product. Qualify FAST and move on.

I'll bet that if you look at your sales pipeline (your entire prospect list and where they are in the sales cycle), more than 40% of those names are a waste of time, especially if they have been in the pipeline for a long time.

If you DON'T have a sales pipeline and you're not tracking exactly where your prospective customers fall in the sales process, you won't succeed. In the absence of data, you will not take corrective action.

If you have examined your sales process with care (see Chapter 3), you already know how long it takes, on average, to close a deal. The average could be two weeks, 30 days, six months, or whatever fits your product or service. If you have a company in your pipeline that is too far outside this close window, chances are you are wasting time.

Most salespeople end up spending too much time on the wrong people. The competent salesperson long ago figured this out and doesn't fall into the trap. Since she is constantly looking for ways to get out of work (and get back to the fun!), she is more than willing to dump the losers she knows will never close in a million years.

Why do salespeople hang onto prospects too long? Two reasons: ego and not enough prospecting skills.

To be a salesperson, you must have a big ego that can withstand constant rejection. Since you DO have a big ego, you never want to throw in the towel and give up on the sale. Come hell or high water, you KNOW you will close this turkey. It's a matter of personal pride.

Don't let your pride get in the way of making money! The opportunity cost of sticking with an unqualified prospect is very high. In the time you take to close a tough deal, you could be knocking down 10 easy deals! That tough customer prevents you from reaching the thousands of eager customers who are out there waiting for you to call. Trim that pipeline!

The second reason we hang onto prospects too long is that we don't spend enough time prospecting. Most salespeople spend 80% of their time selling and 20% of their time prospecting. The ideal salesperson does the exact opposite: they spend 80% of the time prospecting and 20% closing deals and get better, faster, and easier results.

The ideal salesperson doesn't just do your ordinary, garden-variety, common, typical job of prospecting. They attack the process with pure efficiency and joy!

We live in the Information Age. Abundant resources exist for smart people who wish to use them. The Internet gives anyone access to more information than they can process and delivers it in an instant. Salespeople can profile and select prospects with incredible precision, even down to SIC codes and ZIP codes and email addresses. In addition to the phone, they can use mass marketing techniques, e-mail blasts, and research services.

The effective salesperson doesn't waste his time on people who will never buy from him. He does his research (notice this is NOT hard work) to determine who has a real business need for his product. Who is buying it, where do they live, what else do they buy, how big is their company, why exactly do they buy, when, how, and to solve what need?

From this initial research, the salesperson knows exactly where the low hanging fruit is. Her research can produce a quality list of suspects that past history has shown are ideal candidates for her product.

Turning the suspects into prospects, then qualifying and closing deals is much easier when you know you are dealing with the ideal prospect.

A good salesperson can sell most any product to anyone. A great salesperson can even sell sand in the Sahara. But a truly effective salesperson sells water to people who are already dying of thirst! How hard is that?

Here's a story from one of our recent clients:

We did a project for an internet-based startup company that was marketing an online reservation service to RV campground owners. This company was an Application Service Provider (ASP). They delivered their services over the internet for a fee each time a camper made a reservation. This industry owned approximately 12,000 campgrounds. With a small sales force the question became on whom do we focus the sales effort? Where could we achieve the biggest bang for our selling buck? Who exactly was the perfect buyer for this service?

We did a close examination of the potential target market and determined the following facts:

1. Of the 12,000 campgrounds, about half were state and publicly-owned campgrounds that already had an online reservation system in place.

2. Of the 6,000 private campgrounds, about 3,800 belonged to the largest and most powerful nationwide trade association for campground owners, the ARVC. Because these 3,800 campgrounds had already shown an understanding of the importance of marketing and networking (after all, they did pay to join the association), they would be the best prospects for our services in the first phase.

3. The 3,800 campgrounds in the association broke down into four categories based upon the size of the campground:
   A. Small (1-100 campground spaces)
      65% of total population of 3800
   B. Medium (100-250 campground spaces)
      20% of total population of 3800
   C. C. Large (250-500 campground spaces)
      10% of total population of 3800
   D. D. Mega (500+ campground spaces)
      5% of total population of 3800

4. We conducted further research by telephone survey to a focus group which included equal distribution among each of the four sizes of campgrounds. We examined factors in varying categories such as current adoption of technology, feelings about doing business online, current systems in place, size of staff, and location of park. We intended to determine which of the campground sizes would be MOST receptive to the services this company wanted to sell.

5. The telephone polling and research indicated that BY FAR the best campground size to which to sell services were the small and medium sized campgrounds. They had the most urgent need for the reservation service and they were not likely to have a competing system. Further, the decision makers were readily available and the time to close sales was much quicker. The larger campgrounds had remote owners, management by committee, large staffs to consider, and installed base systems.

6. Further research narrowed down the small/medium campgrounds into the six most likely states to focus initial sales efforts upon.

7. We developed and launched a sales plan with excellent results.

Without a specific analysis of the target market, this company could have wasted time and money trying to sell their services to the wrong customer. Instead, they focused on the RIGHT customers and made the campaign a success.

Non-salespeople can use this principle to their advantage in multiple ways. For example, consider the task of achieving entry into a top university. Every student knows that having excellent grades and extracurricular activities is a prerequisite for admission. However, the most successful applicants spend time researching their target market and understand who the decision makers are. They also know the critical decision criteria going into the process.

Knowing this information, the clever applicants build additional proof that they should be admitted over all others based upon criteria they know in advance will be valuable. Most importantly, they figure out a way to sell this value to the people that actually make the final decision.

For instance, they might know in advance that this particular university has an active and powerful alumni group and that these individuals exert considerable influence on admission decisions. Or they might know that a certain university is actively searching for candidates with a particular ethnic background or candidates from foreign countries. Or perhaps the university gives greater weight to the religious background of the candidates.

The more you know about your target market and the decision makers, the greater chance you have of selling your value to them. In life, as in sales, the same principles apply.

The best salesperson knows to spend her time on customers who already want to buy what she has to sell. To do otherwise would be inefficient and a waste of her valuable loafing time!

Chapter **48**

Select Prospects
Or
What should you do with a prospect that is qualified BUT is not ready to buy?

By Philip A. Nasser

"The people who get on in this world are the people who get up and look for the circumstances they want, and, if they can't find them, make them."
--George Bernard Shaw

Here is the situation: You have just had a discovery session with a prospect and they are very well qualified, that is, they have issues and inefficiencies that your product or service can satisfy very well. They have business problems for which you have a good solution with some likelihood of being able to cost-justify the investment. For instance, they are not able to meet their customer's demands in an area that your product addresses or they need tracking information about supplier shipments and your product is able to provide it. You get the idea. The prospect is well qualified, but the problem is they are not in a buy cycle at the present time. If they were, you would grade them highly in your pipeline and activate a sell cycle immediately.

What do you do with this prospect? One of the best salespeople we know introduced us to the select prospect idea. One thing we recommend is to ask the prospect's permission to make them a select prospect. This is a non-threatening way to partner the prospect and put him into a more open-minded and receptive mode by keeping him out of critique mode. Here's how you might do it (of course, feel free to adjust this to your own style so you are comfortable with it):

> "Based on the information you've provided me, it seems your company is a logical candidate to take advantage of our products and services sometime in the next few years or months. Would it be all right if I make you a select prospect? This means:

- I will send you information on an ongoing basis about advances and trends in our products and services that affect your industry. This could be a case history, articles of interest that might include new uses of technology, ways to better serve your customers, advances in your area of specialty, or how to work better with your suppliers through automation, advances in customer relationship management, and so forth. (This needs to be customized to the prospect/industry you're dealing with)
- Also, I'll keep you informed of other companies in your area or industry who purchase our products or services.
- I'll phone you every four weeks or so to see if anything has changed. If nothing has changed, this will most likely be a short call.
- Periodically, I'll invite you to webinars/seminars that we hold in a non-pressure environment where you can learn more about (the industry, your company's solution to customer problems, your specialty, etc.) that may be of interest to companies like yours.
- If I'm in the area, I'd like to be able to stop by for a short visit to form a relationship so you keep us in mind when you think of making a change from your current way of doing things.

You see (Mr. Prospect), our experience shows that companies frequently make decisions on (your products and services) with inadequate information and generally in a hurry, without sufficient research. Many times they wait until just before a crisis occurs to make a decision regarding what they will do. With a decision as important as this, we believe you should have all the latest and relevant information.

We want you to be as well informed as possible so you won't have to do a lot of research or hire a consultant when you make the decision to change (from your current way of doing things). And we'll be able to provide this information over a longer period of time in a calm, non-pressure manner so you won't have to rush to gather or analyze pertinent information. Of course, we selfishly hope that when you make a decision to buy, you'll be more likely to think of us and our chances of securing your business will be improved."

You might ask, "It sounds easy enough, but why else would I want to use this approach?" One key reason is it provides a way for you to differentiate yourself and your company's offerings.

Consider this. All salespeople try to convince prospects that their company's products and services are better than those offered by the competition. Sometimes this is difficult to do. For example, in the case of commodity products you are most often forced to differentiate on something other than product, frequently price and service. You might say something like, "We provide a complete, turn-key solution with the best customer service. We are a customer-oriented company." Unless you have demonstrably better service and customer orientation, and can prove it, you can see how the prospect might be skeptical about your claim. It sounds very much like sales fluff, doesn't it? And doesn't everyone hear enough of that on a regular basis? You need to find other ways to prove you are different and, therefore, better. *The select prospect approach is one great way for you to differentiate yourself from the competition.*

Do your competitors have a select prospect system? Likely not! Would you like to be included in such a program by one of your suppliers or vendors? Likely yes!

Reminder: you must make monthly contact with every select prospect. No exceptions! Since email is so ubiquitous, the U.S. mail is becoming a better alternative. If time allows, a handwritten note accompanying the document you are sending is even better. Other items to send include success stories (yours or your suppliers), articles about your supplier/business partners, annual reports, and earnings statements. Working with your other team members, you will be able to come up with additional items to send. The critical point is you _must_ touch each select prospect every month.

As noted above, the select prospect program also gives you an excellent opportunity to build a relationship and credibility with your prospect. In your many touches over time, you'll be able to make new contacts inside the prospect company, gather additional information on business problems, and gather personal information such as special interests, hobbies, non-work activities, family information, and more. (Of course you enter all this information into your database for future reference and use.) In doing this you naturally build a relationship and credibility.

Chapter 49

Maximize Your Trade Show Investment

By Mark L. Friedman

Trade shows are a wonderful way to generate qualified leads for your sales force. Prepare for them properly and your company will find them to be very cost-effective. Don't plan properly and your company will find them to be a pain in your back and feet and a waste of time and money.

According to recent trade show industry research, over 70% of all leads generated at trade shows are never followed up by sales. Talk about a prescription for disaster.

To illustrate this point, several years ago one of our clients told us this trade show horror story:

The company had spent a lot of money to attend the annual industry trade show; they paid extra for a prime location and had high expectations regarding their lead generation targets. They had a lot of booth traffic and managers were pleased when it was over. They packed up their booth and sent it to storage. The next year they started preparing for the trade show and unpacked the booth only to discover that all their leads had been left in the drawer of the booth and nobody had missed them!!

In my discussions with other trade show exhibit companies, this is not unusual. These companies report that they often receive calls to retrieve the leads from their booths and send them to the company.

Don't let this happen to you! Here are some steps to optimize your investment in your trade show and generate a positive ROI.

1. Take a proactive approach to identifying the ideal prospects that will attend the show. Send a pre-show mailer inviting targeted attendees to your booth.

Recommended process:

- Contact the show producer as soon as possible to ascertain whether a pre-show attendee list will be available.
- Identify what demographic/other criteria are available to segment the pre-show attendee list, if any.
- Create an interesting/compelling offer to attract your targeted

attendees to your booth and include it in a direct mail piece.
- Conduct a telemarketing follow-up campaign focusing on capturing valuable account profile information and inviting the account to your booth.

2. Create a Trade Show Inquiry Qualification Sheet to assist in efforts to quickly qualify anyone who comes to your booth. The trade show will more than likely make available a badge/card-scanning machine. This will assist your efforts to capture valuable demographic information quickly and in electronic format. The Inquiry Qualification Sheet will provide some of the customized information your company deems important in qualifying these inquiries.

For example, in our work with material handling companies, we recommended they include questions regarding the size of their warehouse, the number of SKUs managed and whether they use trucks or conveyor belts. For a client in the computer networking industry, we made recommendations regarding the number of networked devices, the number of computer centers and what operating system they used. Best practice is to work with sales to identify four or five critical pieces of information that contribute to the identification of a qualified lead. These questions are usually not included in the standard information found on the badge.

In addition, while these prospects are at your booth, make a special effort to confirm email addresses.

You won't be able to complete these Inquiry Qualification Sheets for everyone who comes to your booth, but, when you have time to use them, you will receive more information that you can provide to your sales reps.

3. Consolidate all inquiry information from the Badge/Card-scanner, the Qualification Sheets and business cards received and create a single Excel spreadsheet/database. Remove any identified duplicate records and have an administrative resource type in any comments found on business cards or other pieces of paper. Often comments are found on the paper printout from the card scanner system.

4. Import the consolidated attendee list into your Sales Force Automation (SFA)/Customer Relationship Management (CRM) software and make sure to consolidate any duplicate records here as well. If a record already exists in your database, compare the new information and determine what to keep, delete, or overwrite. Make sure to indicate that you made the contact at the Trade Show.

5. Perform literature fulfillment within 24 to 48 hours after the attendee came by the booth. Provide customized salutations and information based on the data collected at the trade show. Special note: many companies have found it much more cost effective to not provide expensive catalogs and other literature at the trade show. It is amazing to look at how many people take this literature and then toss it either on the way out of the trade show or before they get back to the office. This is a big

waste of money. Bring only a few datasheets that have your company/product information and promise to send the customized information in which they expressed interest quickly to their company address.

6. Distribute qualified leads to the sales reps based on pre-determined business rules.

7. Provide a list of all other inquiries to the sales reps and see if they want to contact any of them on their own. What we find is that the field often has targeted a specific company and hasn't made headway in the sale process with their current contact or they have targeted a company but didn't have a contact there. In any event, allowing the sales reps to cherry-pick accelerates and gains more commitment for the post-show follow-up. The sales reps flag those accounts they wish to keep in the SFA/CRM software.

8. All inquiries not flagged by the sales reps should then be contacted with a telemarketing call to qualify and determine interest in further contact with your company.

9. All accounts deemed to be qualified but not yet interested at this time should be flagged for an on-going nurturing campaign. Your company should create a consistent email campaign to send to these accounts that highlights the benefits of your products and/or services.

Conclusion

This comprehensive approach to sales lead management will ensure your company maximizes your trade show experience and generates a positive ROI for your investment in time, money and resources.

Chapter 50

The Forty Pound Phone

By Philip A. Nasser

"It is more than probable that the average man could, with no injury to his health, increase his efficiency fifty percent."   *--Walter Scott*

The forty pound phone sounds like a toy doesn't it? It is not, unfortunately, a toy. It's a business tool and it's reasonably weighty. The forty pound phone we're talking about is any business telephone that seems to be too heavy to pick up and use for its intended purpose, to conduct commerce. The phone sits in its cradle waiting to be picked up and used. Many times it isn't. Why do people have call reluctance? In this chapter we'll attempt to answer this question and provide ways to overcome this malady.

There are many incentives to overcome call reluctance. Pressure for improved sales force performance continues to grow. Quotas increase every year with sort of a wink and a nod from bosses acknowledging that they know we can get more done in the same amount of time. But can we? If so, how do we improve our sales and prospecting efficiency? Is your reason for not using the telephone that you can't get through to the person you called? Or do other things get in the way and you end up not making the call or calls? If so, don't feel bad. You're not alone.

In a minute, we'll look at some ways to overcome call reluctance and, in the process, become more proficient. But first, a case can be made that the best way to qualify a prospect is with a face-to-face meeting. Agreed. The problem is that it has become very costly to travel to prospect locations. With the latest increases in the cost of fuel, all forms of travel are more expensive. Estimates are that it costs a company $500-$1,000 fully burdened for one person to make an in-person call and that assumes there is no out-of-town travel involved. If the call is made out of town, meals and lodging alone, excluding transportation expenses, add an additional $450 in major cities in the U.S.

180

Assuming you can't meet in person with your prospective customers, what is (and has been for decades) the best tool for qualification and communication? Among your possible answers could be:

- Email
- Letters
- Various hand-held communication devices and PDA's
- Text messaging
- The telephone

While all of these tools are good, we believe the best tool is, without doubt, the telephone. It alone has the full set of characteristics. It:

- Is personal (human voice)
- Occurs in real-time
- Is most often one-to-one
- Allows inflection and emotion
- Can be highly effective

It is a wonderful tool to create productive qualification and communication with prospects. The other forms of communication lack one or more of these key characteristics. For example, emails in particular can be impersonal and give you no feedback from the recipient. You cannot make necessary adjustments in content and direction like you can on the phone.

One more related point. We find from working with our clients that it is easier for salespeople to avoid the telephone than in previous years because there are so many additional ways to communicate with prospects. Most of them are convenient and less time-consuming and certainly not as painful.

Still, the major problem standing between salespeople and using the telephone more effectively is the same today as in the past: finding an effective way to overcome call reluctance. One of the first problems encountered is fear of the real pain (rejection) the telephone causes, especially when it is being used as a prospecting tool. None of us likes rejection and, if our egos are at all fragile, this can be a big problem. Intuitively we know this pain is uncomfortable and want to avoid it. We say to ourselves:

- "Why call? Most people hate to have their day interrupted by salespeople."
- "It's impossible to get through anymore. You get stuck in voice mail or are diverted by the secretary or gatekeeper."
- "It's so hard to find a qualified prospect using the phone anyway."
- "I have so many other things to do that are important. The phone can wait."

If we're able to overcome the first objection, and it can be tough, other reasons not to call (more sophisticated objections, you might say) creep into our consciousness:

- "It's about 8 a.m. Most prospects are in early morning meetings and will not want to be disturbed."
- "It's about 10 a.m. This is when business people are the busiest and definitely don't want to be disturbed by a salesperson."
- "Its lunch time and this is a bad time to call."
- "I don't like to have my work interrupted repeatedly all day? Neither does anyone else. No wonder they are sometimes short with us on the phone."

Let's assume through sheer courage you get past these powerful psychological resistances and are ready to call your suspect list. This is when a third set of reasons not to call surface. They are:

- "How will I handle the introduction during the call?"
- "What's my reason for calling?"
- "What value do I bring to the company?"
- "How do I phrase it perfectly to provide the best impact?"
- "How will I cope with rejection?"

The winning approach - the key to overcoming call reluctance - is to have:

1. A plan
2. Clear call objectives
3. Confidence based in knowledge
4. Good discovery questions available
5. A compelling value proposition for the person on the other end of the line.

Following the suggestions below will improve your sales productivity by as much as 200%. They overcome call reluctance, improve your phone skills and efficiency and, most importantly, get you back on the phone.

1. **Have a call list ready.** Doing so will ensure you don't waste valuable time locating the list or lead source from which you will call. With CRM systems, you can load names to call or names can be put into a task list.
2. **Forward all your incoming calls** during the time you plan to be on the phone. You may want to change your voice mail message to say that you will return the incoming calls by a certain time.
3. **Set goals and keep score.** For instance, how many completed calls (a call where you are able to secure one piece of qualifying information) do you want to make? How many inefficiencies do you want to identify? How many qualified prospects do you want to

find? How much time on the phone today will you devote to achieving these goals?

4. **Get pumped up!** Do whatever you need to do to get your energy up and your competitive juices flowing.

5. **Visualize success** in advance of every call. Review the call and have a successful outcome in your mind before you dial.

6. **Is this a good time to talk?** When you make contact with a prospect, we have found it effective to ask if this is a good time to talk. After hearing the question, the prospect may hesitate for a second or two, but most often they let you continue the discussion. If the prospect says "yes," proceed with your discovery. If the prospect says "no," ask when a good time might be to have a five to ten minute phone call.

7. **Establish credibility.** It is important to establish credibility quickly. Many respected sales authors suggest that you only have a few seconds at the start of a phone call to do so. In the first 20 seconds of the phone call, introduce yourself by saying something like "this is _____ with _____ and the reason I am calling is _____." This sets the purpose of the call up front, which executives much prefer to being asked, "How are you?" which is almost always interpreted as insincere.

8. **You've solved this before.** Share with the prospect that many executives have expressed frustration with a particular problem (preferably an industry-specific problem this prospect is likely to have) and that your company has been able to help other companies in their industry solve that problem and that you would like to share with them how it was accomplished. Be ready with your success stories (see the next item below) in case the prospect says something like, "Tell me who you have helped and how they benefited from what you did."

9. **Success stories** are among the best sales tools that sales people have. Prospects need to know that other companies have had success using your product or service. A success story from a company in the same industry almost always interests the prospect. The success story should follow this format:
    - Situation – status of the company when you started working with them
    - Major Inefficiency – the main pain point(s) along with the reasons it/they existed; why they had this problem.
    - Your solution – this succinct description of your solution and its outcome should include specific, measurable benefits that accrued to the client through the use of your solution.

10. **WIIFM.** Have several success stories ready to share with the prospect. You need several just in case the prospect says they don't have the problem you just described. Remember, WIIFM: what's in

it for me. Prospects want to know how they can benefit from giving you time on the phone (or anywhere, for that matter).

11. **How do they handle similar problems?** After a description of the success story, transition directly into your discovery by asking how they handle the problems that your solution removed for your success story customer. *This is the most important section of your phone call since it is here that you determine if the prospect is, in fact, a prospect for your products or services.* Construct your discovery questions perfectly to gather the necessary qualifying information to determine whether this prospect has problems that make them a candidate for your services. Your discovery questions must be targeted at the major inefficiencies in your prospect's organization that your solution will remove.

12. **CEO's Favorite topics** – If you reach a CEO or any other senior executive, know what they like to talk about the most. For them, revenue growth, increased market share, or improved profits can all measure success.

   - At the top of the list is their company's success. Do your homework. Check their web site to find relevant press releases or earnings information.
   - Success for the company is followed closely by success for themselves. Here again, the company web site is a good source of information about the accomplishments of senior executives.
   - Customer service - CEO's and senior executives are always interested in how to enhance customer service. If, for instance, their web site speaks to their mission of providing excellent customer service and your solution helps improve customer service, this is a natural area to do discovery.
   - Competition - staying ahead of competitors is a key success driver for all companies. If your prospect is losing ground to competition, a question about how they are responding to the competitive threat can be appropriate *if* your solution can help overcome that shortfall.
   - Measurable, tangible results (bottom line) – If your prospect is very profitable, congratulate them. If, on the other hand, your prospect is experiencing difficulty delivering strong profits and your solution would help close the gap, a question about the actions being taken to turn the situation around is appropriate.
   - Key measurements – If a key initiative of your prospect is growing their customer base and your solution will help accomplish that, questions about their goals and how they are doing against those goals are appropriate. Ideally it will open opportunities for you.

You need helpful questions that are unique to your solution. The industry you serve will have its unique requirements so customize questions to meet those particular needs. Below are sample discovery questions that help you learn about and qualify a prospective organization.

- What are your plans for the future?
- How do you plan to achieve your future goals?
- Is there anything you are missing that could help you achieve your future plans?
- What's important to you about making a change now?
- What stopped you from considering this change previously? Last year?
- Are there internal resources available that could supply the missing pieces?
- How could you support that initiative with internal resources?
- At what point would you decide to move to an outside partner/vendor?
- How would you know when it's the best time to use an outside company?
- What criteria would you use to choose the outside partner/vendor?
- Have you had experience with outside firms in the past?
- Has anything stopped you from using outside resources before?
- How did you make that decision previously?
- How would you know that my company could satisfy your needs?
- What is the next logical step for us now?

Prospect phone calls generally produce three outcomes:
1. Not qualified
2. Need more qualification information
3. This is a qualified prospect.

In the latter case, what should you do when you intercept a prospect just starting or in the midst of a buy cycle? The answer is to activate the prospect immediately by saying, "I'm really glad I called. We have many customers like you. I'd love to show you how they're _____ (improving efficiency, providing better service, retaining customers, improving profits). May I come out to see you?" Alternatively, "Could we schedule an hour phone call so I can learn more about your operation and how we might be able to help?"

Call reluctance is normal. The more successful phone calls you make the easier it is to overcome this affliction. Get on the phone. Use the tips provided here to improve your efficiency. Here's wishing you the best of luck in your sales career.

Chapter 51

Sales Stages: Funnel, Opportunity, Deal, or Pipeline

By James W. Obermayer

Once the lead is sent to the salesperson, it goes through a filtering process that will either kill it as a prospect or advance it to the next level of the pipeline. You can have just a few stages or a dozen or more. Every company and its products are different. Here are the basic stages. You can always add others.

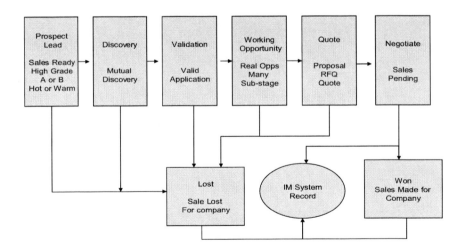

- **Sales Lead, aka Sales-Ready Lead.** This is a qualified inquiry. They have an immediate need, a budget, a projected time frame for purchase, and usually have reached a few other custom thresholds, making it is a genuine sales lead.
- **Discovery.** Many inquiries never get past the discovery stage. This is where the salespeople and the inquirers decide whether they

want to work together and if the products fit the need. Discovery happens during the first few meetings, where the prospect and the seller size each other up and flesh out the problems. This is where the chemistry so vital to a successful sale starts. Otherwise, the future deal dies here.

- **Validation.** At this stage the proof of concept asserts itself. Whether through a demonstration, free trial, free sample, Web seminar, or reference checks, validation is where someone says, "Yep, I think this will work the way we need it to."

- **Working Opportunity.** Just what it says, this lead is being worked by the sales representatives and may become a sale or at least move to the proposal stage. An opportunity is most often those names that are transferred into the sales rep's contact system (**SFA**). These are the leads that appear in the salesperson's forecast. At best 50% of these leads make it to the forecast. The huge mistake many companies make is dumping all inquiries into the **SFA** system and then trying to manage the database, which is bloated with irrelevant names and information, at the salesperson level.

- **Proposal.** Whether it is a quote or a proposal, one page or 50, somewhere in the process you will have to give a number to the buyer. Every company should know the closing ratio of its proposals. Once that proposal is laid on the prospect's desk you should know within a narrow percentage what your chances are.

- **Negotiation/Sale Pending.** Maybe we're slicing this too thinly, but some companies know that the negotiation stage can take time. Once in this area the outcome is reasonably predictable. Unless the salesperson has not done his homework or the two companies have not properly identified serious outstanding issues, the outcome should not be in question; only the final value and terms and conditions are being discussed.

Chapter 52

Sales in the Dumpster?
28 ways to help you dig
to the bottom of the sales panic!

By James W. Obermayer

Sales is a process; control the process and you control your future. The following are 28 questions I ask my clients to review when they are in a sales jam. There are hundreds of places to look for lost sales, but these 28 solve a lot of my customer's problems.

1. **Killed your momentum?** If sales go into a slump, look to your company's actions and find out what your company did or did not do three to six months ago. Common momentum killing mistakes are: changes in sales incentive plans, territory reorganizations, senior management changes, premature product deaths, promotional programs sliced to contribute to the bottom line (talk about an oxymoron).

2. **Change the incentive compensation?** Check and see if management has made changes to the incentive compensation plan. Move the food dish and salespeople will start trying to figure out how to make a living. Only make incentive compensation changes at the beginning of the year.

3. **Lost sales reports?** Find out why you are losing sales; make lost sales reports mandatory. If you don't have lost sales reports, start. It's never too late to find out why you're losing more than you're winning.

4. **Old proposals?** Go back to every proposal (or a statistically significant sample) that you have given out in the last six months and interview the customer to find out why sales are down. Why didn't they buy from your company? Was it price, the salespeople, delivery, features?

5. **Sales lead follow-up?** Look at sales lead follow-up over the last three to four months. Is there a problem? Why has follow-up dropped off?

6. **Resellers playing you for a fool?** Is your channel using your leads to sell another company's products? Do a mystery buyer program. Call your independent sales channel and see who they recommend for your products. Fire those that don't recommend you.

7. **Sales territories turning over?** If your salespeople are resigning, you have to find out why and stop it cold. Every time a salesperson leaves a territory, you create sales leaks for six to nine months. Keep a bullpen of salespeople ready to fill open sales territories or use a recruiter.

8. **Unrealistic quotas?** Is the sales incentive bar set too high? If so (usually visible if very few make quota from year to year), you have to tell the quota-setting president that these high, non-motivating quotas are killing performance. Setting goals that are 30% to 50% higher each year are unrealistic and demoralizing.

9. **Salespeople making quota?** If too many territories are not making quota, ask the salespeople why? I know that's obvious, but try it anyway. You'll be surprised.

10. **Sales incentive systems too complicated?** Ask 10 salespeople how they get paid. If they know how much they'll make by selling your products, you're doing OK. If they can't explain your incentive compensation plan, you don't have one.

11. **Monthly, quarterly and yearly quotas?** If you don't have monthly, quarterly and yearly sales quotas, you aren't running a sales organization with salespeople. You've got a group that will hide behind the group when sales fail to deliver. Set monthly and quarterly achievement quotas and watch sales increase within three months.

12. **Check with inquirers that are less than six months old.** When a group of leads are six months old, 56% are usually still in the market. Go back to them. Love them and nurture them. Bring them to life.

13. **Getting salespeople in front of the prospects faster than your competitors?** Because 10% to 15% of the sales from inquiries are made within three months, you're losing sales if the salespeople are slow to get in front of the prospects. Get your salespeople in the door first and let them set the table for others to follow.

14. **Does the inside sales group get the same sales training as outside representatives?** From getting sales skills training to product training, too many inside salespeople are not treated like outside representatives.

15. **Are there activity quotas that contribute to goal attainment?** Activity quotas are habits and actions that when repeated often enough will lead to a predictable sales outcome. For instance, number of cold calls per day and number of live appointments per week.

16. **Risking too much with hockey stick sales performance?** Hockey stick performers deliver sales in the last week or two of a quarter. If a majority of the salespeople do this, 50% of more of your sales will come in during the last two weeks. This puts pressure on shipping and creates undue risk if the performers don't perform. Pay bonuses monthly for making quota and stop this risky practice.

17. **Tracking the sales pipeline?** Do you know the ratio of proposals or outstanding quotes in the pipeline to closed sales? Do top performers have a bigger pipe? Do you factor the pipeline dollars to be able to predict the future sales?

18. **Are district and regional sales managers risking as much as the salespeople?** Is the sales incentive plan for sales management mirrored to the plan for the salespeople? The closer you get management aligned with salespeople the better and more consistent your results will be.

19. **Are the sales coaches (regional and district sales managers) spending enough time with their salespeople?** Are the coaches shouting from the sidelines or are they in the field listening and coaching salespeople to excel?

20. **Where are the salespeople spending their time?** Have you measured hour by hour where salespeople are spending their time? Is it in the office, behind a windshield, on service problems, on the telephone, in meetings, or in front of new prospects? Make changes to increase the face-to-face selling time.

21. **Do you know the customer's buying process?** How does your customer buy? What are their steps? How many touches do they require to be comfortable enough to sign the purchase order? Do your processes match their steps? Are you in sync or out of sync with their processes to buy your product?

22. **Do you have defined steps to the sale for your products?** How many touches and steps does it take to make the sale? Are your steps different from the customer's buying process? You have to know the customer steps in order to control the sales process.

23. **Open sales territories?** Open territories can silently kill sales force productivity. If you have 50 salespeople (600 months of sales time) and you turn over 10 territories a year and lose an average of six months per territory you have lost 60 months of selling time. Plug that hole with creative hiring, maybe a recruiter to reduce risk and time, add thirty months back into the sales productivity column and watch sales increase.

24. **Is there someone in charge of sales other than the company president?** You have to grow up and put a professional sales manager in charge of the salespeople. Salespeople need care and attention. Inside salespeople need more care and attention than

outside salespeople. Both groups need a daily dose of coaching. If you have a part-time sales manager you'll get part time results.

25. **Weed the garden or accept mediocrity!** Change is difficult. It is time-consuming to replace salespeople. Are you ready to accept the round of interviews, training, coaching and traveling needed to get the best? Are you too lazy to hire the best and the brightest? Are you weeding the garden?

26. **Testing salespeople for sales skills before you hire them?** Many sales aptitude tests will help you reduce your hiring risk. Use them for every new hire. Trust the tests when they tell you a person isn't right for your products or marketplace.

27. **Is lead flow consistent?** Does a salesperson get three leads in one month and forty the next month? Inconsistent inquiry flow leads to boom and bust reactions. Many serious buyers may get flushed because they had the ill fortune to inquire in a month that delivered too many prospects to their local sales representative.

28. **Do you have a sales lead management system in place to track follow-up of leads and marketing productivity?** How do you address the needs of your future customers? Do you track how the salespeople follow-up on inquiries? Are marketing campaigns judged on their successes based on sales produced?

Chapter 53

You Want Publicity?
Here's How to Get It

By Judy Key Johnson

Publicity can bring huge benefits to a company by generating sales leads, triggering introductions to potential partners, employees, and investors, and raising the morale of company staff.

Public Relations (PR), that is getting your company coverage in the editorial (non-advertising) section of newspapers, magazines, e-zines, and blogs, is often seen as free because by definition the publication is not paid to run the article (although pay to play tradeoffs such as ad space for a free article or advertorials blur the line between editorial and advertising).

In truth, getting PR takes know-how, planning, money and other resources because the competition for it is very stiff. A business reporter for *The Orange County Register*, a mid-sized newspaper in Southern California, recently said he receives about 300 press releases a day. Perhaps 20 of them make it into the daily paper either as a two-sentence announcement of a new company executive, a three-paragraph filler or one or two full-length feature articles, complete with photographs.

These tips on how to get publicity come from my experience working at three daily newspapers, a stint in IBM corporate communications, and a decade of hiring PR firms and providing PR services.

Rule 1. Know your target

A common mistake for businesspeople inexperienced in PR is to try to get an article, any article, placed with the first publication that comes to mind. That's a bad idea for a number of reasons. For starters, your odds of success are lower if you haven't first established a plan and followed the rules below. Also, as the saying goes, "Be careful what you wish for, because you may just get it." If you get your new product announcement placed in one trade journal, you may well have ensured that a larger, more prestigious journal won't touch your story. Newspapers and magazines all want an exclusive over their direct competitors so they frequently will not run an article if it's already run in a competitive publication.

With PR, like everything else in business, the "Ready, Fire, Aim" approach doesn't work.

You need a PR plan, which covers an extended time, up to a year, includes all the stories you want placed and flags the ones that are time dependent. Separate the story ideas into categories such as straight news announcements, feature articles, and thought leader pieces. Create a list of publications that might print them.

Next, place your list of media outlets into categories like local news, national news, industry journals and e-zines. Research each potential target publication individually for the types of articles it generally runs and doesn't run. This way you avoid the mistake of pitching a feature story to a trade journal that only runs advertisements and news briefs.

Each media outlet has a set of competitors it wants to beat to newsworthy articles. Know who these competitors are for each publication. Some types of stories, such as news briefs, may be submitted to all media in a group. However, for big feature articles select one target publication in each group and pitch the story as an exclusive. Approach a competitor only if you are turned down by your first choice.

Creating a PR plan requires all the strategy and sophistication of creating a sales plan. Be sure to consider messaging, timing, competition, and packaging. Using a PR firm is a helpful way to jumpstart the process, but most editors will work with business people who pitch their own stories.

Rule 2. Make it easy to say yes

As you research each target publication, create a spreadsheet that documents its parameters. Include the types of articles it runs, from news briefs to full length features, story length, opportunities for photographs or other graphics, writing style, and use of free-lance or staff writers.

Your job is to submit articles, photographs and other materials that mirror the format a publication prefers. Editors are very busy people, so the less work it takes to drop in your submission or assign a reporter to the story, the greater the likelihood that they will accept your idea. Be sure to designate a single, informed contact on your press release to make it easy for an editor to get a quick response to any questions.

Most publications list submission rules online. Follow them.

Rule 3. Remember, it's not about you

A major mistake many PR amateurs, especially business owners, make is to lose sight of the fact that a publication's goal is to publish information of interest to their readers. Articles should be objective, fact filled, and, yes, may discuss multiple sides of an issue and raise uncomfortable or even unflattering issues.

Before talking to a reporter, think about what that professional questioner is likely to ask, especially the hard questions. Don't be defensive. Think of information that will interest all readers, not just industry insiders.

Remember it's about the readers; it's not about you. If you want to control the message, buy an advertisement.

Rule 4. Persistence pays

As with sales, drumbeat PR works. A PR plan should cover at least a year and include frequent submissions, monthly or at least quarterly. Repetition will make your company name familiar to editors, and familiarity inspires confidence if you are following the other rules of professionalism suggested here.

Getting the order, or in this case getting an article published about your company, is partially about being visible and top-of-mind when the publication has space to fill, such as when a story drops out at the last minute or the publisher sells several more pages of advertising and needs editorial copy. The editor sees your article. It meets the submission guidelines and is easy to work with. This is just the break you need.

Rule 5. Connections matter

You've followed the above rules, but you can't get your articles published. Competition is very stiff for editorial space in publications.

It's time to check your contact database and see if you know anybody who can get you an introduction to the right editor or reporter. That's often fairly easy with trade journals; the publisher will be actively involved in trade associations you may belong to. Newspapers are more difficult because story decisions are generally made by the section editor. Other reporters or editors rarely interfere with such decisions.

Consider hiring a PR professional to place an article in local newspapers. Their staff is generally well connected with editors and reporters and knows how to pitch stories for maximum interest. PR firms generally require a retainer and a multi-month contract. Some freelancers will work on a per-article basis.

PR is not rocket science and you can do it yourself. However, the experience and contacts of a PR professional will raise the odds of success. Weigh the return on an investment in PR as you would any other marketing investment. A favorable feature article in the local business press often creates many business opportunities.

PR – A unique opportunity

There is no other forum that can achieve for your company what PR can do, which is to bring the credibility of independent professional journalism to a corporate message. PR has provided tremendous opportunities for companies and also created difficulties where the message is negative. With planning, persistence, and salesmanship, you can succeed in the PR world.

Section Nine

Sales Lead Management/ CRM

Now that your Business Development Engine is cranking, you're probably being flooded by hundreds of inbound inquires and leads. Like most companies, you're probably buried under the sheer volume of incoming communications.

Today prospects can touch you in dozens of ways: phone calls, emails, web inquiries, surface mail, trade show cards, referrals from partners and affiliates, responses to marketing campaigns, from blogs, from social and business electronic networks, from associations and organizations. You get the idea; the list goes on and on.

The job of tracking "who's on first" has never been more difficult. After customer data is entered into your system, who needs access to it? How do you manage your sales pipeline? Who decides what information is relevant? Who is the information distributed to, and when?

All these questions need to be answered and the answers need to funnel into your Customer Relationship Management System. The days of managing your pipeline with a simple Excel Spreadsheet are long gone. They vanished around the time that dinosaurs became extinct.

It you're not using electronic databases and tracking systems to DRIVE NEW REVENUE to your business, I can guarantee that your competitors are! If you're not adopting the latest, the most sophisticated, and the most workable means to manage your leads and customers, you will be out of business within five years or less. Guaranteed!

It's hard to stay current with this technology!

That's where we can help. Read the next section to get a primer course in the modern science of Sales Lead Management.

Chapter 54

Research Supports the Importance of Sales Lead Management

By Mark L. Friedman

According to several recent Business-to-Business (B2B) company research studies, effective Sales Lead Management pays off big time, not only in increased sales and profits but also with increased business valuation for an exit strategy.

Operational Research

A Forrester Research study found that firms in the top tiers of their Sales Lead Management Maturity Model enjoyed better sales, higher follow-up rates and closed a higher percentage of marketing-generated leads.

Of those companies that fell within the top two tiers, 46 percent report that sales reps follow up on 75 percent or more of marketing-generated leads and 35 percent of companies close 10 percent or more of leads. Of those companies falling within the lower two tiers, only 28 percent of companies report that sales reps follow up on 75 percent or more of marketing-generated leads, and only 19 percent close 10 percent or more of leads.

Netting it Out

Top–tier companies close almost twice as many leads as lower-tier companies. What are the consequences for your company?

The study then showed that B2B marketers can no longer afford to emphasize lead volume against lead quality. This practice reduces sales efficiency, increases costs, and fuels the gap between sales and marketing. Does this sound familiar?

The Velos Group recommends evaluating your current unique business processes to identify how to optimize the handling of all inquiries and leads to ensure that no qualified leads drop through the cracks. Once these processes are designed, map them onto your Sales Force Automation (SFA) or Customer Relationship Management (CRM) software.

Through the aggressive use of this software and monitoring the progress of all qualified leads, your company will head down the road to increased lead follow-up and Sales Lead Management top-tier status.

Exit Strategy Research

A survey commissioned by Sage Software reveals that small and mid-sized businesses must use their customer relationship management (CRM) database as a tangible asset and a differentiator to obtain the best value from their business as an **exit, succession,** or **transition.** Having customer data in a single CRM system is a valuable asset according to 70 percent of respondents with exit strategies. Having a central record of all customer relationships is a significant business and financial asset for companies seeking an exit, whether the exit strategy is a trade sale, succession, venture capital funding, or public offering.

According to Sage Software, having a CRM system provides a strong negotiation tool to maximize the value of your business because it provides any future owner or manager with insights into the customer base and opportunities. This allows them to hit the ground running and minimizes disruption to customer service.

The Velos Group strongly recommends the creation of a centralized, customized Customer and Prospect database with a comprehensive Account Profile built in. Once created, the company should import newly generated inquiries and leads along with existing prospect and customer information. The company should then ask the sales reps to provide the company with all relevant information from company-generated inquiries, leads, prospects and customers.

Once collected, this information should also be imported into the database. It's okay to ask for all sales rep contacts, but be aware, if the company did not generate the initial information most sales reps will not provide the information to the company. Some might, but don't expect it. Incorporate application security to grant sales reps the access privileges they need, but no more, and make it more difficult to export or delete important company information.

Once the database is up-to-date, all information regarding customers, inquiries and leads should be entered into the database first. By doing this, the information in the CRM database will become a valuable corporate asset and will increase the company's value.

Additional Company Valuation Perspective

As we discussed above, managing your sales leads, leveraging the value of your customer base and using your Sales Force Automation (SFA)/Customer Relationship Management (CRM) more effectively can all contribute to increasing a company's overall value. While sometimes considered to be mostly tactical in nature, we are beginning to recognize the strategic importance of implementing best-in-class Sales Lead Management techniques.

Many methods are used to determine the value of a company:
1. Market Replacement Value – the value of comparable businesses
2. Income – historical, current, and projection of company's profits
3. Asset Value – the value of the company's assets

Quality and performance of the management team is an important factor in each method when evaluating the worth of a company. Repeatability, consistency, process, procedures and proven systems are all signs of a superior management team and contribute to the increased valuation of a company by investors or buyers.

In traditional manufacturing, the business value of process is well understood. People know that the value of an automobile manufacturer is not based on the ability to produce a single, high-quality car. It is based on the reliable and repeatable ability to create hundreds of thousands of high-quality cars at a predictable cost. Companies that apply the same discipline to their Sales Lead Management process demonstrate significant sales and profit growth and outperform their competition on a regular basis.

A company with proven Sales Lead Management processes, procedures and systems will demonstrate the following over a long period of time:
1. Increased sales results
2. Increased sales productivity
3. Increased predictability of revenue and profits
4. Increased consistency of revenue and profits
5. Growth of customer base
6. Accurate, tightly-controlled Central Database of customers and prospects (Managed as a company asset, company not held hostage by sales reps – what if they leave the company)

Conclusion

Effective Sales Lead Management and Customer Relationship Management increases sales results and sales productivity and also positions the company for a higher valuation. Increased consistency and predictability of revenue and profits with a solid customer database in place is the key.

Chapter **55**

Why Most Sales Lead Management Programs Fail

By Mark L. Friedman

Most Sales lead Management Program implementations fail because:
1. They lack management support/follow-up.
2. The program is too complicated to administer and use.
3. They lack a Closed-Loop System Approach.
4. They focus on Quantity vs. Quality: Inquiries Not Qualified.
5. Qualified leads not distributed in a timely manner to lead owner.
6. Feedback regarding lead status is difficult to collect.

Lack of Management Support/Follow-Up

An entire constellation of services and human connections goes into building a successful sales lead management project. This assumes, first of all, a company-wide strategy to be best in class in its sales processes and procedures. Without that, most lead management procedures and activities will be empty gestures that do not produce results. Once a company makes that real commitment, from top to bottom, then it must design functional activities and re-engineer work processes to be genuinely efficient, fast and effective. Only then does software technology come into the picture. In short, successful sales lead management is NOT software.

The statistics are sobering. Approximately 75% of Sales Force Automation and sales lead management programs fail to meet the expectations that were used to justify the project. By far the biggest reason is that upper level management, although approving the budget and expecting the project to be a great success, does not participate in the user requirements sessions and does not communicate as forcefully as possible that this IS the way we will be doing business in this area. As Jay Curry, a CRM expert and author of a couple of books on the subject, put it, "If the owner/CEO is in charge of, or monitors closely, CRM implementation and processes, then the good news is that he can get done what he wants to get done. However, if he loses interest, it's all over."

The program is too complicated to administer and use.

Another common failure of implementing systems like this is that they are designed at a corporate headquarters, often with a "Wouldn't it be great if we could...." mentality. What happens next is that a three to four inch-wide System Requirements Document is created and many, if not all, nice to haves become hard must-have requirements. It is absolutely crucial to start with the end in mind, but equally important is to keep in mind that a sales rep demands a system that makes his job easier and more productive AND is easy to use. Each of the hard must-have requirements should be evaluated using these criteria and then prioritized so that only the most important requirements are addressed, at least in the first phase of the roll-out. Other requirements that don't get prioritized as highest can be implemented in successive phases as long as they will make the sales reps more money, make the existing process easier to use or produce better management reporting (without creating an extra burden on the sales rep.)

Lack of a Closed-Loop System Approach

If a company's current system can be classified as "Catch as Catch Can," then we highly recommend the company apply the same systems/process-driven approach that their manufacturing and quality departments have been using to this critical business process. The dividends gained will be more than worth the work put into it. The Sales Lead Management process begins in the Marketing department then flows into the sales organization. The information gathered in the Sales Force Automation systems provides the input to several important departments within the company. It is crucial that each step of the process is mapped with an eye towards:

- What is my overriding business objective?
- Is this the most efficient way to handle this process?
- How does this process contribute to the achievement of business objectives?
- Where are my inputs and who receives the output?
- Who needs to be involved to ensure that cross-system and inter-organizational coordination is considered?

This planning and business process review becomes more complicated and involved based the level of integration a company desires in all of its major business systems: manufacturing, financial, inventory management, customer service, and sales. It is a big job and requires a great deal of thought, but it is absolutely critical in designing a best-in-class system that will become a strategic advantage and contributor for the company.

Focus on Quantity vs. Quality: Inquiries are not qualified leads.

If a company's objectives are to improve sales force results and productivity, it is imperative that the company start qualifying sales inquiries and only pass along qualified leads to sales. The more gross calendar content time sales spends in front of qualified prospects, the more successful they will be in achieving their targets.

It is critical to separate the inquiry qualification job function from the selling to qualified prospects function. This can be accomplished with an internal group located in either the marketing or sales department or it can be outsourced to another company, such as a telemarketing agency. In either case, the key to success is a commitment to qualifying all inquiries based on criteria agreed upon by sales first and marketing second and then closely monitoring the results of each marketing activity.

Once the company has committed to making this fundamental shift in approach to Sales Lead Management, they can start measuring the quantity AND quality of each inquiry and marketing activity. Over time, the company will be able to determine which activities produce the most and best leads for sales and which contribute to the successful attainment of sales goals and market share goals. As companies become more efficient in the allocation of their marketing budgets, they will see a corresponding increase in their bottom line.

For example, for one client I implemented a closed-loop system and produced a report that highlighted some interesting things that helped the company spend their advertising money better:

1. The trade magazine that produced the most number of inquiries was actually producing the fewest number of qualified leads and thus the highest cost per lead and, as we found out, the highest cost per sale.
2. The publication that produced the fewest number of inquiries actually produced a disproportionately higher number of qualified leads and sales.

I'm convinced that if the company had not implemented the Sales Lead Management program, they may have spent their advertising money differently and would not have been as effective.

Qualified leads are not distributed in a timely manner to lead owners.

Good, qualified sales leads are a lot like a good piece of fish; they're better fresh. The longer they lie around, the worse they get. While it is good to qualify each inquiry and only distribute qualified leads to sales, the method and speed with which this is accomplished is a critical element in the success of the Sales Lead Management system. The basic problem most companies face is that they use an hierarchical organizational approach and require a human to make decisions as to which sales resource will address the lead.

Successful companies document their lead distribution rules and then incorporate them into their Sales Force Automation software. As a result, once a lead is qualified, it is automatically distributed to the ultimate lead owner. All individuals in the organizational chain are info copied or told how to view the information within the SFA software. It is important to design, document and manage the process of exceptions where no clear-cut lead owner exists.

Fast distribution and quick follow-up by the sales organization results in the prospect having a better perception of the company, the sales rep gaining a better opportunity to shape the specifications of a potential solution and, as a result, generation of more sales at a higher gross profit margin.

Feedback regarding lead status is difficult to collect.

In the past, companies have provided Sales with their inquiries or leads in one system (paper, email or Excel spreadsheets), told them to work their leads in any system they feel comfortable with, and then required their pipeline/forecast reporting in another system.

The Sales Lead Management system should successfully eliminate these multiple systems. Properly constructed, it is one unified system requiring very little extra effort by the sales rep to create the advantages for which the system was designed:

- Fast distribution of sales leads
- Increased sales results and productivity
- Creation of actionable management reporting which helps to manage the business more effectively and efficiently

Once the system is in place, a sales rep must be required to update the status of the accounts they are working with, which then serves as the input for the Pipeline or Forecast reporting. Everything else is handled by the software and requires no sales rep involvement.

Chapter 56

Sales and Marketing Can Love Each Other: Six Steps to Creating the Best Sales Leads

By Mark L. Friedman

The relationship between Sales and Marketing typically can be a challenging one. Sales leads are often at the heart of the problem. Marketing executes an advertising or direct mail campaign or manages a trade show, then delivers a bunch of unqualified inquiries (which they usually call leads) to Sales thinking their job is done. Sales takes the leads, makes a few calls to qualify them only to find out that most are not interested or their target customer type. They look at Marketing NOT as a helpful partner in the sales process and as not interested in supporting the company's sales quotas. Marketing then receives feedback from Sales that their leads were no good and is suspicious of the sales department's ability to know a good lead if they fell over it.

As dismal as this sounds, there are ways to break down these barriers. By following six simple steps, Sales is guaranteed a steady stream of qualified leads and Marketing has the information they need to gather better market intelligence AND track ROI for each program in the marketing mix.

1. Identify the ideal prospect profile.

The best prospect for a company's product or service can be found by mining its customer database. Skillful analysis of current customers' (and often prior customers') demographic characteristics can help a company target companies with a similar profile. Even companies who have not collected this type of information in a disciplined manner can exercise database techniques to perform a rudimentary analysis of their customers.

By gaining a better understanding of the customer profile, it is then a straightforward exercise to work with list brokers, trade magazines and other sources to find and acquire names of companies that match the target customer profile. The advantage of performing this segmentation analysis is that a company will spend less money purchasing lists of companies that do not match their profile, can do a better job evaluating which publications are their best advertising vehicles, and determine which trade shows match their target customer demographics best. All this additional information leads to a more efficient expenditure of marketing funds in programs with a higher probability of generating *qualified* leads for sales.

2. Look to Sales for useful marketing information.

Marketing listens to Sales regarding how they approach these accounts and what messages get them in the door to advance the sales process. This real information is invaluable in helping Marketing revise their messaging and positioning statements in the marketplace. They will also gain a better understanding of the competitive landscape.

The sales force is also a rich source for recommending product improvements or new options that prospects and clients want. All this helps Marketing assist Sales in their efforts and drives a more symbiotic relationship between both groups.

3. Agreement on What's A Qualified Lead

Marketing and Sales need to agree on the criteria for a qualified lead. It is critical that Sales be involved in determining the criteria by which an inquiry is qualified as well as defining what a qualified lead is. Only then will the leads from Marketing be given the attention they deserve and be followed-up on quickly.

When Sales receives non-qualified inquiries, their natural reaction is to ignore them. Why? A recent study may shed some light. A sales inquiry company analyzed millions of inquiries from many industries over a period of years. The analysis revealed that only 30% of all inquiries proved to be sales leads. Of that small group, 10% were hot leads, 40% were warm leads, and the remaining 50% were future leads (those leads that are not yet at a stage in the buying cycle to be worth personal attention).

4. Marketing qualifies all leads first.

Marketing should qualify all inquiries before they are sent as leads to Sales. Although it is an added expense to pre-qualify all inquiries, there is a real cost associated with not qualifying them. Valuable and expensive sales time should not be wasted on the pursuit of ill-defined and poor quality leads. If nearly one-half of all inquirers buy within a year, then, by definition, more than one-half do not.

One study showed that only 12% of all inquiries qualify for a personal sales call at the time of inquiry. The challenge is to distinguish the inquiries that have promise from those that don't. Today's communication technologies and techniques make this a manageable task, but it is a task that should be done by a lead qualification specialist, not by salespeople who do not have the tools, the skills, or the time. Inquiries should be qualified and screened before they are sent to Sales.

5. Sales Force Automation software has a job to do.

Sales must set up the SFA software to define the stages of the sales process.

By doing this, Sales makes it easy for Marketing to track the success of each marketing program and the status of each qualified lead. When Marketing does not receive feedback on the status of the qualified leads sent to Sales, they cannot justify spending the money to generate and qualify inquiries and, even worse, there is no way to determine which programs are working and which are not. This typically results in marketing budgets being slashed since there is no way to calculate the ROI for the money spent, which ultimately has a negative impact on the ability of Sales to hit their assigned quotas.

Part of this process requires Sales to define the various stages in a sale and then make sure forecasts are generated using these sales stages. Once this is done, the Sales Force Automation software can be modified to collect this information and create on-line forecasts and ROI tracking on marketing programs and campaigns.

6. Learn from leads that don't close.

Sales and Marketing need to agree on the nature of information collected about why a lead did not result in business. This information is valuable to both sales and marketing. It can assist in structuring an advanced training program for sales and can point to changes needed in product features and pricing. Both organizations need to agree on the likely entries for each stage and incorporate them into drop-down menus in their Sales Force Automation software.

If these six steps are followed and maintained over time, the sales and marketing departments will find it much easier to support each other's objectives; the company will experience more efficient marketing programs that produce a steady stream of qualified leads and increased sales will result.

Chapter **57**

Common Points of Inquiry Leakage

By James W. Obermayer

Leakage happens because most companies, unfortunately, are not counting all of the inquiries they receive nor are they attributing the inquiries to their proper sources. When this occurs, the marketing department will lose the ability to properly credit the lead-generating campaign that caused the person to make contact. This isn't a small problem, it's a big problem. It's a 10% to 30% problem. Most companies that gain control of the portals of sales lead entry into their company see a 10% to 30% increase in inquiries and qualified leads that can be accurately counted and properly attributed to a campaign. Sales increase.

The common areas of leakage are:
- **Calls to customer service.** Inquiry calls to this group are often thought of as intrusions and irritants. Customer service reps are seldom trained to determine what prompted the inquirer to call. They rarely have inquiry entry screens on their computers for this purpose. Even a paper form for taking inquiry interest is better than nothing. If your toll-free number in an advertisement could end up in customer service, get the operators trained to take inquiry calls. Tell them how important these calls are for the company. Most inquiry management programs, including **CRM, SFA,** and contact management programs, have a section titled *Enter New Inquiry*. Teach customer service people how to use it. Use paper as a backup or a last resort to capture the vital information of an inquirer, including the source.
- **Inquirers (usually callers) that go to a salesperson or local office.** In some companies inquiries are intentionally directed to the local sales office. That would be great were it not for the fact that few of these offices will take the time to attribute the caller to a specific marketing campaign. Instead, the calls should be taken at a

central contact center where the name and information is entered and then hot-transferred to the proper salesperson.

- **Calls to executives or Marketing.** These are often lost for accountability purposes. Sometimes they are given to salespeople; sometimes the questions are answered, but the names and sources of the inquiry are not recorded. Executives can also learn to use the Enter New Prospect screen.

- **Trade show inquiries.** Just because a sales rep speaks to someone in his or her territory during the show doesn't mean that he has the right to pocket the inquiry. Use computer lead retrieval or multiple-copy lead forms at shows and let the salesperson take a copy if it is in their area.

- **Small local shows.** After all, it is a local show. Why send the inquiries to the home office just so the representative can get them back a week later? The reason is that a local show may not be booked next year if the marketing department can't review the total quantity of inquiries and the **ROI** from this year's show. In addition, the prospect may not get the literature they wanted. Again, use multiple-copy lead forms so the reps can separate and keep their own copy.

- **Emails from "Contact Us" Web pages.** Too often the emails that are generated go to someone who will read them and maybe forward them but seldom add them to a database. They are not counted as an inquiry. Maybe the person's needs are met, maybe not.

- **International inquiries.** Too often inquiries from foreign countries are not recorded. If they are, the names are many times not passed to the local sales office in the country or region that handles the prospect. They are lost.

- **Representative-generated inquiries.** One of the most undercounted sources of inquiries is the category called Rep Generated. It can be 5% to 10% of your total inquiry count if you:
  a. Give the salespersons training on why they need to report these inquiries.
  b. Give them an easy-to-use system to enter the names. Again these are entered in the *Enter New Prospect* section of the inquiry management, **CRM, SFA,** or contact management program.

If you look hard enough, you might be surprised how many uncounted, undocumented, un-data based inquiries are lurking in your company. When you find them, both sales and marketing will benefit.

Chapter 58

The Six Ways to Prove that Sales Inquiries Convert to Sales

By James W. Obermayer

Proving that marketing programs create sales isn't difficult. However, this is not to be confused with proving a return on investment. I define ROI as a percent of dollars returned from an investment (dollars put at risk). Here we talk about the simplest ways to prove the conversion rate for inquiries. Are there more than six? Probably, but these will cover most circumstances.

1. Salespeople report: The best way

In this instance, salespeople report on the disposition of every inquiry through your CRM system, SFA contact management program or ASP vendor. If you sell direct, you have the control to make this happen. If you sell indirectly and the company uses an ASP software product or service to track inquires and leads, you're in luck. But if you don't have such a service or program, you'll probably use items three through six.

2. Compare invoices to inquiries: The most accurate way

If you sell direct and have the names of people who buy from you, you can compare the name with the person who inquired. If the sale is made after the inquiry date, you can claim a connection and take credit. If you have multiple contacts with the prospect, I would credit the original source of the inquiry. For instance, you may have gotten an inquiry from direct mail, they subsequently called the company, maybe even responded to an email blast, signed up for your on-line newsletter and stopped by to see you at a trade show. All of these touches contributed to the sale, but without the first touch you weren't even in the game.

3. "Did You Buy Studies" By Telephone. A Statistically Significant Way to Take Snapshots Of Buying Activity For A Single Product

Take a list of inquirers that are six months old and call them. Get at least 100 completed questionnaires from a single product and a single point in time (typically a month) and you have a report that is significant. You will know what percentage buy in six months from you or your competitor. Any outbound telemarketing company can do this for you. Ask questions such as:

- Did you get the literature you requested?
- Did a salesperson from our company contact you?
- Have you bought a product?
- What did you buy?
- Who did you buy from?
- Are you still in the market?

4. "Did you buy studies" by mail

Similar to "did you buy studies" by phone, this method is attractive because it can generate the greatest number of responses at the lowest cost. For every inquiry that comes into the company, send them a self-mailer six months later. Make sure the self-mailer can be refolded so it becomes a return mailer to you. The response you get can be 10-25% over time. Make sure the name is coded so you can compare like sources to like sources within a specific timeframe and you have the most inexpensive study possible.

5. "Did you buy studies" using email

This is an attractive method, although with the email opening rate continuing to drop, you may have a difficult time getting at least 100 responses for a single product and source at a specific time (month). Try it. It is cheap, fast and sometimes very efficient. If you get many thousands of inquiries in a month for a limited product set, you may have a winner here.

6. Comparing warranty registrations to inquiries will give you reliable and statistically significant information.

Compare warranty registrations with the inquiry database and you have a statistically significant report if the date of purchase is after the inquiry date. I recommend crediting the first recorded instance of the person contacting you for the product of interest. This isn't perfect, but it is statistically valid.

Section Ten

Best Practices
In Sales Lead
Management

Managing sales leads is a disciplined process that starts with the end in mind. At the end of the day, world-class companies want to know what marketing programs are best driving sales and profits. To get superior results, track responses and ROI for each marketing program and continuously analyze comprehensive reports of what has changed with their program leads.

With this in mind, we will look at how you can set up a responsive account profile that will guide your lead generation and qualification efforts. This account profile can also unlock the power of targeted marketing and customized communications to your customers and prospects that will reinforce the on-going success of your sales and marketing efforts.

Next we will outline a proven approach to code your inquiries and responses so that you can create reports to determine the ROI for each of your marketing programs. Because so many inquiries are coming from the web, we will discuss ways to make sure you capture these leads and automatically import them into your Sales Force Automation/Customer Relationship Management software.

Once these inquiries are entered into your software, it is critical that they be qualified before sending them to your sales organization. The value of lead scoring is that you will develop a common terminology regarding the quality of the leads sent to Sales that will allow Sales to become more focused on the best opportunities and become more productive as well. We will describe a couple of approaches to lead scoring that any company can use to dramatically improve in this area.

And lastly, generating qualified leads isn't good enough. They must be quickly and effectively distributed to the ultimate sales person who will make the next contact. Since companies face many obstacles in this area, we recommend using business rules and computer technology to immediately forward these leads to their "rightful" owner as quickly as possible.

Apply the lessons from these chapters to dramatically improve sales and profit and ultimately, the value of your company.

Chapter 59

Know Your Customer: Increasing Sales through Spot-on Account Profiling

By Mark L. Friedman

Can you define, very precisely and in writing, what your customers look like? If you can, you have a valuable asset and I hope you're exploiting it to the maximum!

Companies that implement programs designed to generate sales leads are always looking for ways to increase the probability that an account will respond. One of the best ways to increase the response rate is to know what their current customer base looks like – for example those accounts who have responded favorably to previous programs – and try to find more accounts that share their characteristics.

By gaining a better understanding of the types of companies (by size, industry and other relevant criteria) your company has successfully sold to in the past, you can determine which customers should be prioritized in future sales and marketing programs. Additionally, your company will be able to better target companies when purchasing additional lists and/or databases. By targeting prospects that look like their customer base and creating marketing programs that address the same concerns and issues their customers faced and explaining how they solved them, companies will increase their overall response rates.

Create a Best-in Class Account Profile

Creating a comprehensive customer profile is the first step in gaining a better understanding of the characteristics of those accounts. The key to identifying the data elements for this profile is to answer the following questions:

- What information is important to your company in identifying specific groups of customers that have similar needs and finding solutions to address those needs?

- What information is required from the sales organization in order to identify a qualified lead?
- What information does the marketing organization require in order to implement successful lead generation programs?

Once Sales and Marketing have answered, prioritized and agreed upon these questions, use three primary locations and methods to collect the information that will create a responsive Account Profile.

Three Information Sources

1. In-House data

Companies often neglect one of the best sources of information that will populate the Account Profiles – their own customer base. Departments that typically interact with customers – Sales, Marketing, Customer Service, and Accounting – can each contribute valuable information for the Account Profile, such as:

- Key contacts
- Last order date
- Products and services purchased
- Payment history
- Systems information
- Returns history
- Revenue and profits generated

By collecting this information, a company can segment its customer base to deliver specific information regarding new products and upgrades or to make special offers to customers that haven't ordered within a given timeframe. The net effect of these more targeted and relevant communications will be more sales generated with a lower cost of sales.

In addition, several of our clients have used an objective measure of their customers' payment and returns history to help determine pricing for new proposals; the better the overall experience, the lower the pricing. Conversely, if the customer has a history of late payments and higher returns, future proposals will be priced higher.

2. Outside data

By using third party databases, such as Dun & Bradstreet and InfoUSA, companies can augment their in-house profile information with additional valuable data such as:

- Precise industry - (SIC/NAICS)
- Company size - number of employees, annual sales
- Senior contact - president, owner
- Location type - HQ, branch, single location

When combined with the information from their in-house data (see above), a company can identify the top industries and product lines by sales and profits. This analysis will assist the marketing department in designing sales programs that will produce greater sales and profitability.

Gaining a more complete and objective picture of the characteristics of your customer base allows your company to perform more targeted acquisition of databases and lists to better support sales and marketing programs. I have worked with many small to medium sized companies where someone knew this information but had not taken the time to transfer it into a data base environment that would have made it significantly more efficient to identify groups of companies with common characteristics.

3. Lead Qualification Information

As sales inquiries are qualified and while your sales organization is in contact with these prospects during the sales process, specific account information can be captured and added to the account profile. Some examples of specific qualification information for the Material Handling industry, for instance, can be found below.

Size of Warehouse	Number of Trucks
Number of Employees in warehouse	Brand of trucks
Use conveyor systems or trucks	Application - Load/Unload, Storage and Retrieval
Linear feet of conveyor system	Type of products - Case, Individual, Pallets
Number of Conveyor lines	Engine type - Electric, Diesel, Propane, Gas
Number of Shifts	Own or lease trucks

As these prospects become customers, other organizations, such as Customer Service, can be asked to fill in some of the information missed during the sales process.

In addition, this qualification information can help a company determine more objectively whether and how a prospective account should be processed. The closer a prospect matches the ideal account profile, more resources should be used to qualify the account and forward it to sales. A company can also determine the most cost-effective manner to respond to the prospect's request, either a full (and expensive) literature kit or printed catalog, for instance, or an email response requesting more information or with a link to the company's web site.

Where to keep the family jewels?

In order to take full advantage of the account profile to help create successful sales and marketing programs, this information should be found in your company's Sales Force Automation (SFA) or Customer Relationship Management (CRM) software. That way sales, marketing, and anyone else who deals directly with customers and prospects will have access to it when they need it.

It is critical that Sales and Marketing agree on what information they need to qualify an inquiry and what they need to initiate a sales call on an account. Once Sales and Marketing has identified what information needs to be kept in the software, the software should be modified to make sure it contains each data field.

Creating a customer and prospect profile as detailed above will increase response rates for sales and marketing programs. In addition, using the information to better qualify sales inquiries will have a positive impact on sales results, sales productivity and ultimately profitability.

Chapter 60

Coding Marketing Inquiries to Track Sales Results

By Mark L. Friedman

Start with the end in mind. One of the desired end results from a closed-loop sales lead management system is the automated generation of a suite of reports that helps management evaluate the effectiveness of each marketing activity. We need to ensure that all inquiries generated are entered into a marketing database in a planned, consistent manner in order to accomplish this important objective. Only then can a company pull out the information needed to track responses and costs in a manner that allows them to make informed, intelligent decisions regarding how best to allocate their marketing budget.

The first step in understanding how to keep the end game in sight is to agree on and implement a consistent coding scheme for all Marketing activities within their marketing database/Sales Force Automation system (and share this with Accounting). This will create a more consistent reporting structure and will allow each stakeholder, whether sales, marketing, accounting, or customer service, to receive and evaluate information critical to their operation.

There are four specific areas of information that are required to build a successful closed-loop sales lead management system and create a comprehensive marketing effectiveness reporting capability:

1. Campaign Type – this identifies the type of marketing campaign responsible for stimulating a response. For example:

Code	Description	Code	Description
A	Advertising	R	Referral
D	Direct Mail	S	Seminar
E	Events	T	Trade Show
P	PR/Articles	O	Other

The cost per item for generating a sales inquiry or a qualified lead needs to be evaluated in the context of the type of program that generated the inquiry. It is important to be able to compare the cost of generating inquiries and qualified leads within the same type of program as well as to be able to evaluate these costs compared to each of the other program types. Armed with this information, a company can identify the most effective trade show among all attended as well as the most cost effective program among all programs. Management can then make better decisions regarding the appropriate allocation of their marketing budget.

2. Campaign or Project Name – identifies the name of the specific function/project. For example:

Code	Campaign Name
A0401	Advertising; University Ad
D0403	Direct Mail; ISP Mailing, March 2004
T0412	Trade Show; CES 2004

In order to track the effectiveness of each specific marketing activity, it is critical to assign it a unique code or name. When done in this manner, the reporting for each activity can be evaluated independent of its source (see below.)

3. Source – Names the specific stimulus (source) from which an individual response was derived. For example:

Code	Description
TCK	Trade Publication; Computer Week
TNW	Trade Publication; Network World
LDB	List Company; Dun & Bradstreet

Entering this information will give a company a report on how many inquiries came from a specific source and which specific ad or list source generated the inquiry

4. Response Vehicle – Defines the response medium through which the respondent contacted the company. For example:

Code	Description	Code	Description
01	800 call to company	06	FAX
03	800 call to agency	07	In Person
04	Magazine Bingo	08	Other

When creating a reporting capability, it makes sense to keep the response method separate from the source. A company will be able to determine, over time, which response methods produce the most and best-qualified leads. Decisions can then be made regarding which method to use when qualifying the leads.

In addition, when it comes to literature fulfillment, this information can be used to determine which types of responses and which response methods receive a full literature kit, a partial one or an email response only. This helps a company reduce its expenses and still allows them to respond quickly to an inquiry.

NOTE: It is very important to note that an inquiry generated from the web typically has a trigger mechanism (a direct mail piece, a magazine ad or an email solicitation). Requesting the trigger source will provide more valuable marketing information as opposed to recording the inquiry as a web hit.

Some examples will illustrate the power of identifying a specific response:

Example Code	Description
D0405SCM02	Q104 PC Memory Upgrade Mailer. Source: CMP, Via BRC
T0402MTM07	Network Interop Trade Show Feb 2004. Source: Company database. Via: In person
A0401TDM01	Q12004 Tea Cup Ad. Source: Data Communications Via: Web
A0401TDM05	Q12004 Tea Cup Ad. Source: Data Communications Via: BRC
D0410MAT02	April 2004 CPU Upgrade Mailer Source: D & B Via: Call to company

The Marketing department is tasked with entering this detailed information into the prospect database in order to track the effectiveness of each marketing activity. When the sales force sees this information, however, it should be in a more easy to understand format such as Q1 2004 Memory Upgrade Mailer. This gives the sales rep a better idea on how to prioritize the lead and approach the prospect

Whether using a code based approach or a more intuitive text-based approach, the critical step is to create a consistent coding scheme that allows the company to generate consistent, accurate, sophisticated and detailed reporting. The objective of this reporting is to track the effectiveness and return on investment (ROI) of each marketing program and to assist the company in more effectively allocating its marketing budget. By analyzing the results and taking appropriate actions, marketing will generate more and better leads for sales. The company will then drive sales and profit growth more efficiently and effectively.

Chapter **61**

Integrating Web Inquiries into Your Sales Lead Management System

By Mark L. Friedman

A recent study conducted by Performark found that nearly half of web site inquiries were never answered in spite of the fact that the companies had paid to advertise their web address in full-page ads. What's worse, of the 30 percent of the company web sites offering downloadable materials, only 25 percent of them attempted to gather qualifying data about the site visitors. Aside from potentially costing your company a lot of revenue and profit, poor Web design also creates a very disappointing first impression of your company. After spending the money to drive interested people to your web site, you don't want to drop the ball on initiating your Sales Lead Management program.

The following steps will help you take full advantage of the visitors to your web site and ensure that your sales lead management system is immediately implemented with little or no manual intervention.

1. Offer valuable information or a compelling offer that will be of great interest to a prospect.

The key is to offer something of interest to your potential clients, preferably something they can't get anywhere else.

Here are a couple of examples. One of our technical recruiting clients offered a White Paper entitled *Industry, Occupational and Demographic Trends through 2008*. Another client offers a free subscription for access to a sub-set of a large proprietary database.

What about a compelling offer for products or services from your company?

2. Require the visitor register to download the information or receive the offer and include several mandatory qualification questions.

Both your Sales and Marketing departments have requirements outlining the type of information that should be requested from a web site visitor.

Marketing is attempting to find out where a visitor heard about the company and other market dynamics.

Sales must know if there is an immediate need they can satisfy or whether a budget has been established. For it to work successfully, Sales and Marketing must agree on the questions asked and also how they are prioritized. Sales should be realistic about the minimum elements required to identify an account as a qualified sales lead. Marketing should understand the ways and sources available to gather the marketing data they need.

Once these questions have been prioritized, we suggest that the company experiment with the number of mandatory questions their web visitors will answer in order to receive the information offered. Web site statistics will indicate the percentage of visitors who don't complete the form. The goal is to capture as much high-priority information from as many visitors as possible. Each industry and company has different dynamics regarding their web visitor experience and tolerance and different offers and information have different response metrics.

Experiment, track your data and remember, as soon as you find a combination that works, it will probably change after a while, so keep tracking!

3. Create an automated process to determine the lead quality.

Let's be honest, not every visitor who lands on your web site looking for information will be a qualified lead. Once the sales qualification criteria have been established, whenever possible provide a drop-down menu from which to select and agree upon a standard measure of a lead's quality. We often look at two main components:

- Revenue potential of the opportunity or company
- The decision timeframe

Depending on the answers to these two questions, most companies can quickly judge the quality of the lead.

4. Create an automated process to determine the ultimate sales lead owner.

This can be a bit tricky if a company hasn't given this issue a lot of thought. Companies often arrange their sales organization hierarchically by geography and sometimes by product. Among the many ways to organize a sales team are a field sales group and an inside sales and channel sales group.

You get the picture. It is important to document which salesperson will ultimately be responsible for working the lead and contacting the interested party. The better the business rules are identified, the easier it is to use the computer to automatically assign the lead. One of our clients identified four levels of logic before they were able to identify their ultimate lead owner, but once they did, the program assigned it automatically.

As part of the process, ensure that each management level within the organization can see which sales lead the program has assigned to a sales rep in their group. In addition, after all this is done, design a procedure for those accounts with no ultimate lead owner that will identify them in your system and manually assign one.

5. Create an automated response process.

This process should incorporate Business Rules based on the answers from the registration form. These rules should include:

- Produce interest
- Company type (end user, consultant, etc.)
- Lead quality (to determine response type and information to be included)

The goal is to send a customized email response immediately or to fulfill the request through the mail within 24 hours if necessary. In addition, based on the lead quality, a company may decide to send a full literature pack through the mail or they may send an email with the requested information as an attachment. This will enable the company to reduce expenses while still responding quickly.

6. Automatically import data into your existing Sales Force Automation (SFA)/Customer Relationship Management (CRM) software.

All of the registration form, lead quality and lead owner information must be imported and routed to the ultimate lead owner. Develop a procedure within this software that notifies the owner that they have a new lead. You can program some software to send an email and some will automatically create a task that will appear when the sales rep logs into the system. The net result is that the lead owner can react very quickly to a new lead.

Success Story

By following the steps above, your company can effectively manage the visitor traffic to your web site and immediately provide sales with the best-qualified leads. Sales results and sales productivity will increase. In addition, you will enhance the prospect's initial experience and impression of your company.

In a recent engagement, one of our clients, utilizing several different sales partners, was generating in excess of 150 web leads per day. These leads were not managed very efficiently, contributing to a significant lack of productivity in the inside sales group. Working with Cerius Interim Executive Solutions, Inc., the client made some minor changes to their web forms and started collecting relevant sales qualification information consistently from each source.

They sent this information to a database, where the lead quality and ultimate lead owner was determined. Once determined, every 60 seconds the records were imported directly to a sales rep's calling list. Since the lead quality was already identified, they could prioritize their calling and could refer to all the information from the registration form. The result was a significant increase in calling productivity and sales closes. The last time we checked in, the client was generating more than 200 Web leads a day and easily handled the increase with their existing staff. **And sales were up over 40%.**

Chapter 62

Not all Leads are Created Equal – the Value of Lead Scoring

By Mark L. Friedman

We all know by now that we need to train everyone in the Sales and Marketing organization to follow up on all qualified leads quickly and efficiently. However, we also know that not every qualified contact/account is going to make a decision at the same time and that some leads represent larger revenue potential than others. In addition, not every contact is the decision maker. So what is the best way to communicate how hot, how big and high up the decision making tree the sales lead represents? The answer is to create a lead scoring methodology and lead quality code that is universally recognized and understood throughout the Sales and Marketing organization. For those companies selling through indirect channels, each channel partner needs to understand what the lead scoring and lead quality code represents as well.

Lead scoring is a method of classifying a sales opportunity by either assigning points or creating a lead quality code based on responses from qualifying questions. Since every company is unique in the way they approach their sales process and the markets in which they compete, these scores need to be customized to provide optimal value to the organization.

What is the value of lead scoring?

1. Determine whether the lead should be forwarded to Sales or to a reseller, retained for cultivation/nurturing, or not pursued at all.
2. As qualified leads are sent to Sales, they will have a better way to prioritize their follow-up activities.
3. Decisions can be made regarding the most cost-effective way to fulfill these inquiries. The Lead Quality field can be used to determine which ones (when the information is captured with the inquiry – trade shows, Business Reply Cards, web leads) should be sent email responses, CDs or full-literature packs. This will reduce costs and still allow fast response to all inquiries.

4.   It becomes possible to track the number of inquiries from a marketing program plus the number of qualified leads as well as the timeframe and size of these leads. As more information is tracked over time, the marketing department can evaluate which activities are generating the best leads and which activities need to be expanded, modified or eliminated.

Lead scoring can be relatively straightforward and incorporate just a couple of key criteria to produce a lead quality code.

For example, I worked with a client who specialized in providing moving services to corporate clients. We set up the following lead quality code approach where the revenue potential was based on the estimated number of annual corporate moves/adds and office configurations. The results looked like this:

Decision Timeframe	Revenue Potential
A = 0 – 3 Months	1 = 500+
B = 4 – 6 Months	2 = 350 - 499
C = 7 – 12 Months	3 = 250 - 349
D = 13+ Months	4 = 100 - 249
	5 = 25 – 99
	6 = 1 – 24

The Lead Quality Code in this case is a combination of these 2 digits, for instance, an A3 or B2.

As you become more sophisticated with your lead scoring, the best practice is to design a scoring system that values all leads above a certain point level.

Here are the steps we recommend taking to establish a lead score:

Step 1: Identify those key qualifying criteria that identify the best leads (ones that typically result in more sales success). For instance, budget approved, industry, company's employee size, product interest, installed systems information, identified need, decision timeframe, revenue potential, and decision role of contact.

Step 2: Identify the relative importance for each criterion and assign a maximum number of points per criteria.

Step 3: Within each criterion, assign the number of points for each response received.

Step 4: Determine a total score to determine whether a lead should be sent to sales, kept in marketing for further nurturing or not pursued.

The results might look like this:

Active Project: Total Possible Points: 30	
Response	Number of Points
Yes	30
No	10

Budget Approved: Total Points Possible: 25	
Response	Number of Points
Yes	25
No	5

Number of Networked Devices: Total Possible Points: 20	
Number of Devices	Number of Points
1,000+	20
500 – 999	18
250 – 499	15
100 – 249	12
50 – 99	10
1 – 49	5

Project Timeframe: Total Possible Points: 15	
Timeframe	Number of Points
0 – 3 months	10
4 – 6 months	15
7 – 12 months	5
13+ months	0

Decision Role: Total Possible Points: 10	
Decision Role	Number of Points
Decision Maker	10
Recommender	8
Member of Team	5
Information Gatherer	0

The maximum number of points is calculated. In this example, it is 100. Marketing would then identify the point at which a lead is considered qualified and send it to Sales. Less qualified leads would be kept in Marketing for further nurturing or not pursued. The scoring approach is then communicated to all sales and marketing personnel who might receive the sales inquiries or the qualified leads.

You can use many other criteria based on your company's unique requirements. You should keep this approach flexible. It can be applied to different product lines or vertical markets, based, once again, on sales input. In addition, it is important to revisit the scoring approach each year or whenever market conditions change.

Conclusion

The value of this exercise is that Marketing now has a clear idea of Sales' expectations regarding which leads should be sent to them. Sales is now assured that the leads sent to them fit their requirements and is much more committed to following up on them as well as providing feedback to Marketing regarding their sales status. Additionally, Marketing starts to gather valuable information on which programs are generating the best leads and ultimately the most sales. When this happens, a company will experience increased sales, higher sales productivity and an ability to allocate their scarce marketing resources to those programs that are working best for them.

Chapter 63

Sales Leads Are a Lot More Like Fresh Fish Than Fine Wine!!

By Mark L. Friedman

Two recent studies indicate that the process of sending qualified leads to a company's sales organization is fundamentally broken.

In the first study, it was found that 70% of all Trade Show Leads are never followed up by sales. All the time, effort and money spent attracting people to the company's trade show booth was wasted. In addition, a second study conducted by Performark found that the company took over 60 days to follow up on 60% of Business-to-Business leads.

Over the years, numerous advertising studies have consistently indicated that when companies inquire about one of your products or services, 20% of them end up purchasing from someone – either you or your competition - within six months. 45% end up purchasing within 12 months.

What is the implication for your Sales Lead Management program?

Speed matters. The first company to respond to a qualified lead stands a better chance of closing the deal. This is why sales leads are a lot more like fresh fish than fine wine; sales leads do not age well! It is critical that a company optimize their processes to quickly and efficiently respond to qualified leads.

There are a couple of important reasons for this:

1   **Image enhancement** – when you respond quickly and professionally to an inquiry, the account perceives your company as organized and responsive. "That's the kind of company I want to do business with," they think.

2   **Influence the specs; close the business** – Responding to an inquiry quickly and qualifying it effectively will uncover potential buying opportunities. Often, if you are early enough in the prospect's buying cycle, they will be receptive to working with your company to understand their requirements in depth and are

open to receiving recommendations regarding what to look for or what product/service features should be included in a buying decision or bid document. Once this happens, the company will use your information to not only to define their buying requirements but also will evaluate responses according to your coaching and the information you provided. As a result, you dramatically increase your chances to make the sale.

Why are qualified leads not routed in a timely manner? Lead Distribution can be complicated, especially in larger organizations.

Many companies employ a segmented sales strategy, assigning different sales personnel or teams to specific groups of prospects:

- Fortune 1000, government, education, etc.
- By product line
- Current customer base, new business
- Accounts handled by direct/indirect sales channels

In addition, many sales departments are organized in a well-defined hierarchical and/or geographic manner. In these organizations, leads are typically sent to the cognizant sales director or sales manager, who is then asked to determine which salesperson in their territory is best suited to handle the lead. This introduces potential delay into the system as the sales manager may be traveling, on vacation, or just not available to route a hot lead in a timely manner.

In organizations that qualify all sales inquiries, the contact and qualification process can take a long time, especially if a large number of inquiries are received in a short period of time. Without bringing on additional resources to help qualify these new inquiries, a significant amount of time can pass before a qualified lead is forwarded to the sales organization.

Using a systems approach, these elements of speed need to be optimized in your Sales Lead Management process:

1. **Speed in responding to the inquiry** – establish a goal to respond in one manner or another within 24 hours whenever possible. This can be with an auto-responding email, customized to an inquirer's product interest or company type. If possible, collect enough information from the inquirer to determine the most cost effective method of response, whether it is an email, literature pack or a phone call from a real live person.

2. **Speed in qualifying an inquiry** – responding to an inquiry is the first step. Incorporating a mechanism to qualify the inquiry, based on established criteria received from the sales organization is the next step. Companies should strive to accomplish preliminary qualification for web leads whenever possible by constructing forms that ask basic qualifying questions. Otherwise, either a

person from your organization or from an out-sourced agency should accomplish inquiry qualification. Be sure to have enough resources to accommodate both the average number of inquiries received on a weekly or monthly basis plus the expected spike anticipated from Trade Shows and other marketing campaigns.

3. **Speed in delivering qualified leads to the ultimate lead owner** – Once an inquiry has been qualified and it meets the definition of a qualified lead, it is absolutely crucial to deliver this lead to the ultimate lead owner as quickly as possible. This seems like a relatively easy thing to do, yet many organizations struggle with this part of the process.

Best practice calls for a company to create business rules that identify the ultimate lead owner in their sales organization or in their indirect sales organization and use Sales Force Automation (SFA) or Customer Relationship Management (CRM) software to automatically assign the lead to that owner. It is critical that Sales provides the input for these rules. If there could be multiple ultimate lead owners, define the preferred methodology to distribute the leads. Typical schemes involve a Round Robin approach or a first come/first served approach, where the potential sales reps are the first to accept or respond to the lead.

In addition, it is important to define an exception process: If the Business Rules can't identify a lead owner, identify the resource(s) within your company that will be the final decision maker for the lead assignment. Have the lead delivered to that resource and track the time it takes to assign the lead. Once a decision is made, use the SFA/CRM software to notify the lead owner AND determine whether the Business Rules can be modified to make an automated lead assignment decision for any leads that match the criteria.

Once a lead has been assigned, the company can either rely on the SFA or CRM software to notify the lead owner that they have a new lead or the company can call or email the lead owner to check their software for the new lead.

The real issue is that unless a lead is immediately delivered to the correct ultimate lead owner, the inevitable delay lessens the chance of your company making the sale.

About the Authors

Patrick McClure, president of the Connexia Group, is a speaker, trainer, consultant, and author who enjoys working with individuals and corporations to help them achieve maximum performance. He is a member of the National Speaker's Association, Toastmaster's International, the Association of Consulting Professionals, and the Global Speakers Forum. He has dedicated his practice to helping others become more successful. To learn more and to receive Patrick's free Newsletter, please visit www.connexiagroup.com or email patrick@connexiagroup.com. Office: (949) 858-0755. Cell (949) 683-7144.

Mark L. Friedman, President of the Velos Group and an industry expert in Sales Lead Management, worked at Shearson Mortgage, Basic Four, Madge Networks, CalComp, Ingram Micro, etc. National speaker and author on sales lead management. Mark can be reached at (714) 544-1003 or mark@velosgroup.com.

Judy Key Johnson, founder of Key Marketing Group, a marketing agency and interim/part-time executive service, is a former IBM sales rep and business executive and president/COO of Southern California technology companies. She combines the discipline and class of Big Blue with the aggressiveness of an entrepreneur. Judy can be reached at (949) 422-8210 or jjohnson@keymarketinggroup.biz.

Philip A. Nasser, Managing Partner of Sales Productivity Institute LLC, has specialized in the information technology industry. He has been a CEO Coach, general manager, VP of Sales, solution selling sales trainer and is known for driving growth in difficult situations where tact and change are needed. He is also a part-time professor of Management at California State University, Fullerton. Phil can be reached at (949) 768-1630 or phil.nasser@salesproductivityinstitute.com.

James W. Obermayer, Principal of Sales Leakage Consulting, Inc., is an author, consultant and speaker. He is also a principal in Cerius Interim Executive Solutions. Obermayer has authored two books, *Managing Sales Leads, Turning Cold Prospects into Hot Customers* and *Sales and Marketing 365*. In addition he has co-authored two other business books and written 90 plus articles for the business press. Over 16,000 copies of Obermayer's books are in print. He is also the founder of the Sales Lead Management Association which has over 1,100 worldwide members. Obermayer works with companies that have sales leakage issues and he is often called upon to fulfill interim sales and marketing executive management positions. Obermayer can be reached at www.salesleakage.com or at (714) 998-1737.